AUTOMANIA

AUTOMANIA

The Complete Book of Automotive Trivia

Alan McPhee

Summerhill Press, Toronto

© 1990 Alan McPhee
Published by Summerhill Press, 52 Shaftesbury Ave.,
Toronto ON M4T 1A2
Distributed by University of Toronto Press, 5201 Dufferin St.,
Downsview ON M3H 5T8
Distributed in the United States by Firefly Books,
250 Sparks Ave., Willowdale ON M2H 2S4

Printed and bound in the United States

Cover design by JAQ
Cover and text photographs courtesy of the
National Automotive History Collection in Detroit
Text design by Nancy Roberts-Knox

Canadian Cataloguing in Publication Data
McPhee, Alan, 1934 –
Automania
ISBN 0-929091-11-6
1. Autmobiles - Miscellanea. I. Title.
TL154.M26 1990   629.222   C90-093654-1

To my wife Linda

CONTENTS

FOREWORD

Five years ago I wrote an autobiography telling my story in the car business, and one thing that took me by surprise is that people were dying to read it.

I know that my controversies at Ford and the drama of turning Chrysler around sparked their interest. But I'm also sure that a lot of people read it because it had to do with cars, and not many things intrigue Americans more than cars.

There have been thousands of books written about the automobile over the years. Most of them are at the Detroit Public Library's National Automotive History Collection. It's the biggest public archive of its kind in North America. Along with books, it contains photographs, sales literature, shop manuals, and owner's manuals. In all, a million different items.

The Library wanted to give everybody around the country the chance to browse through its Collection, and that's what this book does. *Automania* provides snap-shots of the automobile, going all the way back to 1869. Not only is it a valuable source of information, it is also fun and entertaining.

In 1987 I presented a check from Chrysler to the Library to help support and sustain this valuable resource. Now 20 percent of all royalties from *Automania* will go there, too.

So as long as Americans keep buying new cars, the Library will keep collecting memories of the old ones.

Lee A. Iacocca

INTRODUCTION

Nobody invented the automobile. At least no single individual can make such a claim. The passenger car as we know it today took hundreds of years to evolve and the earliest traces are lost in the mists of time, along with the origins of the wheel.

We know that steam power was well understood by the Chinese as early as 800 B.C., and the early explorers and missionaries returned to Europe with many accounts of legendary fire-breathing vehicles. The Jesuit Father Ferdinand Verbiest, who worked in China from 1659 to 1688, left a description of a steam-powered vehicle in his *Astronomia Europeae* which appeared in Latin in 1687.

It seems most likely that Father Verbiest based his description on information he found while working as Keeper of the Imperial (Chinese) Observatory. The two-foot long model he built and described was certainly a viable vehicle, using the fundamentals of a steam-powered turbine, but it did not stimulate any further interest.

Automotive historians accept 1769 as the date for the birth of the modern automobile. At this time, French artillery officer Nicholas Joseph Cugnot designed and built a steam-powered tractor with the specific purpose of hauling large artillery pieces. This vehicle didn't survive its first test run, but a second vehicle — which can be seen today at the Conservatoire Nationale des Arts et Metiers — is the oldest existing "automobile" in the world. It is also, incidentally, the first front-wheel drive automobile.

It would take another 115 years before all the necessary ingredients were in place for the creation of the modern automobile as we know it. The honors go to Gottleib Daimler and Karl Benz who, working quite independently, introduced respectively, the "Sidewheeler" (1885), and the "Gas Engine Tricycle" (1886). This was the real beginning of the automotive age and the world has not been the same since. *Automania* is an attempt to provide readers with a window on that world full of wonderful and wacky inventions, successes, failures, and an endless cast of eccentric characters.

The biggest challenge in attempting a work like *Automania* is in the research. One has to have access to a vast store of information and that information must be credible. I am therefore deeply indebted to Ron Grantz and his staff at the National Automotive History Collection of the Detroit Public Library. This is probably the biggest public collection of automotive information in the world, with well over one million items and more than one hundred thousand photographs, many dating back to the 1890s. All of the photographs in this book are taken from the NAHC files and most have never been published before.

Automania is intended to be an entertaining approach to the history of the automobile and open the door to this fascinating world.

CHAPTER 1 ✹ THE PIONEERS & OTHER BEGINNINGS

There were no automotive engineers in the beginning. Throughout Europe, Great Britain and North America in the mid-to-late 1800s, scores of young men were serving their apprenticeships as gunsmiths, railroad and marine engineers, carriage and bicycle makers, without any inkling that they would soon bring those skills to bear on the fledgling automobile industry. And chance would play a big role.

In the 1850s, the French Royal family re-introduced the crinoline gown to the world of fashion. It was very popular but expensive, requiring whalebone hoops and stiffeners. Steelmaker Armand Peugeot saw an opportunity and responded by developing a technique to manufacture thin, lightweight steel rods which were a cheap alternative to the whalebone. While this was a great success, Armand hadn't reckoned with the fickle nature of fashion. When the style inevitably died out, he was faced with finding some use for his factory. The bicycle boom was just about to take hold and Armand realized that his thin steel rods were ideal for bicycle spokes — voila, Peugeot Bicycles. Immensely successful, Peugeot made the logical transition to automobiles in 1891.

Charles Jasper Glidden "rode the rails" on his historic round the world tour. Where there were no roads, Glidden fitted flanged steel wheels and ran his car on the railroad tracks. In what year did Glidden start the first round the world tour by car: 1904, 1908, or 1911?
1904.

What car did he use?
A six-cylinder 1903 Napier.

The Canadian Pacific Railway would not permit an "automobile" to run on its tracks. How did Glidden solve the problem?
The car was designated as a train and called "The Napier Motor Car Limited". It also had to carry a conductor, named Alex Forrest, and he can be seen sitting behind Mrs. Glidden in the photograph which shows the car arriving in Vancouver after crossing the Canadian Rockies.

Why did Ettore Bugatti bury his latest racing engines under the workshop floor in 1914?
Bugatti's Molsheim plant was directly in the path of the advancing Germans at the start of WWI. After burying the engines, he escaped in two racing cars to Italy. He returned in 1919, recovered the engines and continued the Bugatti legend.

How did a broken jaw lead to the development of the electric self-starter?
Starting a car by crankhandle was strenuous and sometimes dangerous. Byron Carter of Cartercar — a close friend of Henry Leland of Cadillac — stopped to help a stranded lady motorist. The crankhandle 'kicked back', breaking his jaw and causing complications from which he later died. So when Charles Kettering approached Henry Leland with an idea for a self-starter, he received an immediate order for 8,000!

What was unique about the automobiles produced by Italian Michel Lanza in the 1890's?
They were truly unique. He saw each one as an individual work of art and destroyed the moulds and dies upon completion of each vehicle.

AUTOMANIA

In 1903 Lee Chadwick founded a company to build cars bearing his name. Finding coachbuilding firms generally unsatisfactory, he started his own. Chadwick passed into history in 1914, but the name of his coach-building company survives. What is it?
Fleetwood, now part of General Motors.

The Fiat company was founded in 1899. What do the initials FIAT stand for?
Fabbrica Italiana Automobili Torino.

What is the significance of the Fiat motto, "Terra-Mare-Cielo"?
It refers to the company's involvement in land, sea and air activities.

Henry Royce died in 1933. During that year, the company decided to paint the intertwined "R-R" radiator symbol black. What colour was it before?
Red.

Why did they make this change?
Some hold that it was a mark of respect for Henry Royce but there is also evidence that it was done for purely aesthetic reasons.

Henry Ford completed his first car in 1896. What was it called?
The Quadricycle.

Only the French would do it. This cross between a bus and a train, named "Micheline" — note the Michelin tire-clad wheels — ran from Paris to Deauville on rails in 2 hr. 3 min., at an average speed of 207 kph. The body is by Carrosserie Wibault and the car is powered by a Hispano-Suiza engine.

THE PIONEERS & OTHER BEGINNINGS

Henry Royce is supposed to have been prompted to build his first car because he was disgusted by the performance of a French vehicle he had purchased. Was it a Decauville, a De Dion Bouton, or a Panhard?
A Decauville.

What was the price of the Ford Model T when it first went on sale in 1908: $780, $850, or $950?
$850.

Over the next five years, the price dropped to $395, $440, or $530?
$440.

What was the price of the Model T by 1923: $290, $395, or $450?
$290.

Two companies have used "crossed cannons" as corporate emblems. One was French, the other, Italian. What were they?
Hotchkiss of Paris and Ansaldo.

Artillery officer Nicolas Cugnot's 1769 steam tractor, generally accepted as the world's first motorized vehicle, established another distinctive "first" that was certainly not intentional. What was it?
While demonstrating the tractor to the Duke of Choiseul in the hope of securing a military contract, Cugnot lost control and crashed into a wall. Both the wall and the tractor were demolished, and thus became the world's first vehicle accident statistic! He didn't get the order either.

June 4th, 1896. Henry Ford photographed on the streets of Detroit, shortly after the first trial run of his Quadricycle.

AUTOMANIA

In 1901 Austrian entrepreneur Emile Jellinek ordered the whole year's production of sporting Daimlers from the Canstatt company. He felt they were ideal for his wealthy customers in the South of France, but there was one important condition to the sale. What was it?
Jellinek felt that the Prussian name "Daimler" would offend French sensibilities, still smarting from defeat in the Franco-Prussian War. He insisted that the cars be renamed "Mercedes", after his twelve-year-old daughter.

When the Ford Model T was introduced in 1908, what selection of colours was offered to customers?
While most remember only the black Model T, the first year they were also available in green, red, blue and two shades of gray. The following year the colour selection was reduced to only Brewster green with black trim and red striping. It wasn't until 1913 that Henry Ford said, "You can have any colour as long as it's black."

Was the first Rambler a steam wagon, a bicycle, or an electric carriage?
A bicycle. Englishman Thomas Jeffery was a highly successful bicycle manufacturer in Chicago before moving to Kenosha, Wisconsin in 1901 to start automobile production. The Model C was first offered in 1902.

Fill in the missing middle names:
Erret _____ Cord
Lido _____ Iacocca
John _____ DeLorean
Erret Lobban Cord, Lido Anthony Iacocca, John Zachary DeLorean.

One evening in 1906 a reception was held at London's swank Trocadero Restaurant to unveil a new car. Was it a Wolseley, a Napier, or a Lagonda?
It was a Napier.

What was unique about this car?
It was the world's first production 6-cylinder car.

A replica of Cugnot's second steam tractor.

THE PIONEERS & OTHER BEGINNINGS

What was unusual about the hood of the 1908 Cadillac Runabout?
It was a dummy. The engine was under the seat!

In the early 1900s, several U.S. companies designed and marketed vehicles for a specific professional customer. What were these models called?
"Doctor Models".

What did it cost to purchase a Duesenberg J. in 1929: $3,000, $14,000, or $20,000?
$20,000.

How much did Detroit Tigers owner Thomas Monaghan pay for his 1934 model in 1985?
One million dollars.

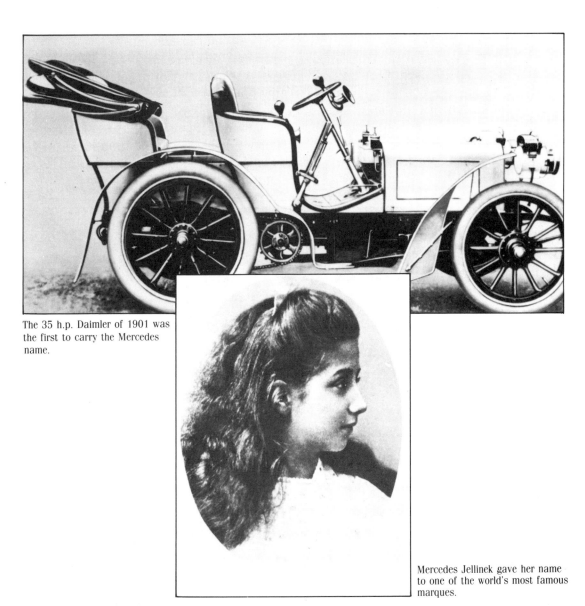

The 35 h.p. Daimler of 1901 was the first to carry the Mercedes name.

Mercedes Jellinek gave her name to one of the world's most famous marques.

AUTOMANIA

What great American car featured a racing greyhound as its hood emblem?
Lincoln.

What company did Charles W. Nash purchase in 1916?
The Thomas B. Jeffery Co. of Kenosha, Wisconsin.

What was Nash's previous job?
President of General Motors.

Two brothers produced the first American automobile in Springfield, Illinois in 1893. What were their names?
J. Frank and Charles Duryea.

What is the origin of the name "Cadillac"?
It comes from the name of the founder of Detroit, Antoine de la Mothe Cadillac.

What was the first mass-produced car in the world: Ford, Oldsmobile or Peugeot?
Oldsmobile. Production began in 1901.

What was the famous Oldsmobile model that launched the company?
The Curved Dash Olds.

Who founded the Oldsmobile Company?
R.E. Olds.

What do his initials "R.E." stand for?
Ransom Eli.

Olds left the company when it became part of General Motors in 1904. What new car company did he form?
The Reo Company.

Henry Ford was "third time lucky" when he launched the Ford Motor Company in 1903. What were his two previous attempts?

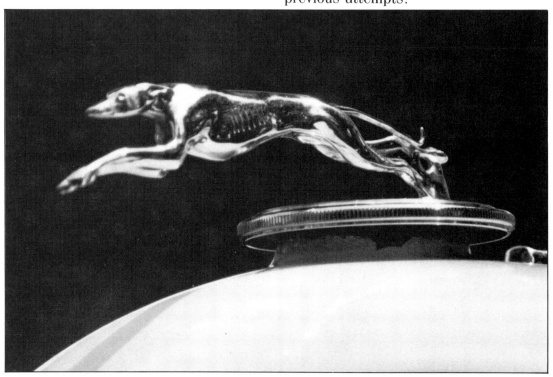

The Detroit Automobile Company which was formed in 1899 and collapsed almost at once, and the Henry Ford Company of 1901.

The backers of the Henry Ford Company, impatient with Henry's inability to produce a saleable car, brought in Henry Leland to re-structure the company, squeezing out Henry Ford. What was the new company called?
The Cadillac Car Company.

Who was the founder of General Motors?
William C. Durant.

What does the initial "C" stand for?
Crapo (a corruption of the French, Crepaud).

When was the company formed: 1902, 1905 or 1908?
1908.

What car company was Durant's first acquisition in 1904?
Buick.

The Buick Company was founded by Scotsman David Dunbar Buick who had made his fortune earlier in a very different manner. What was his previous business?
In plumbing. He patented a process that bonded porcelain to iron, and was used in the production of sinks, toilets and bathtubs.

Name two other companies acquired by Durant in the formation of General Motors.
Cadillac, Oldsmobile, Oakland and some long-forgotten names such as Cartercar, Welch, Marquette, Rainier, Elmore and Rapid.

The classic Duesenberg J of 1929 with Murphy "Clear Vision Sedan" bodywork.

AUTOMANIA

Durant's reckless expansion led to financial trouble in 1910 and GM's bank had to step in and take control away from him. Although still a board member, Durant started again. What new company did he form?
The Chevrolet Motor Company.

By 1915 Durant was able to regain control of General Motors. How did he do it?
In 1910 he quietly started buying up GM common stock and by 1915 he had regained controlling interest.

The Model T Ford was introduced in what year: 1904, 1906, or 1908?
October, 1908.

What were its most popular nicknames?
The Tin Lizzie and Flivver.

What do the letters MG stand for?
Morris Garages.

When did the first Volkswagen go into production: 1936, 1938, or 1945?
1945. Only a few hand-built prototypes were seen prior to World War II.

When was American Motors formed: 1952, 1954 or 1956?
1954.

What two companies merged to form AMC?
Hudson and Nash-Kelvinator.

George Mason of Nash-Kelvinator was named first president of AMC, but he died unexpectedly six months later. Who replaced him?
George Romney.

Romney led AMC to its most profitable years but retired in 1962 to run for what political office?
Governor of Michigan; he won.

The 1934 Chrysler Airflow looks good to the contemporary eye but it was too "far out" for thirties tastes.

The original Kaiser prototype shown at the Waldorf-Astoria in 1946 included one engineering feature that did not survive into production. What was it?
Front-wheel drive.

Before Toyota made cars, what was its business?
The Toyoda Automatic Loom Works.

Toyota's first attempt at a passenger car was in 1935, when they chose to copy a recently introduced American vehicle that featured very advanced styling. What was the vehicle?
The Chrysler Airflow.

The first Japanese company to enter the automotive mass market did so with a Fiat copy in 1917. Later, the same company would shock the Allies with its high-performance Zero (Rei-scn) fighter in WWII. What is the name of the company?
Mitsubishi.

Today Mitsubishi markets cars in the United States under its own name and also supplies them to one of The Big Three. Which one?
Chrysler receives Colts from Mitsubishi.

Chrysler and Mitsubishi also share in a joint-venture production company in the United States. What is its name?
Diamond Star.

What vehicles are produced by Diamond Star?
The Plymouth Laser, Eagle Talon and Mitsubishi Eclipse.

Henry J. Kaiser with his 1946 Special.

AUTOMANIA

What cars are made by Fuji Heavy Industries of Tokyo?
Subaru.

Datsun was the name previously used by Mazda, Nissan, or Toyota?
Nissan.

What do the initials DAT signify?
They represent the founders: K. Den, R. Aoyama and A. Takeuchi.

Models were originally named Datson, but were renamed Datsun in 1932. Why?
So that the company could use the rising sun as its emblem.

What British car company also used the Japanese Rising Sun for its emblem?
Sunbeam. Founded in Wolverhampton, England by John Marston who had a japanning and tinware business. The first car was produced in 1899.

In 1805 American Oliver Evans built a massive steam powered dredge for use in the port of Philadelphia. However, because he had built it some way from the river, he had to mount it on wheels and drive it to work. It thus became the first self-propelled "automobile" in North America, and also the first amphibian. What was it called?
Orukter Amphibolos, literally translated as "snorting swimmer".

When forced by litigation to prove that the Selden Patent applied to a viable automobile, George B. Selden (in bowler hat) had to build and demonstrate it. He is seen here in 1905 with Ernest Partridge, a New York auto dealer, on a test run which proved that Selden was anything but viable.

What was Captain Dick's Puffer?

A crude, six-passenger road steamer built by Englishman Richard Trevithick in 1801. Unable to raise any interest in the road machine, he turned his attention to rails and built England's first steam locomotive in 1804.

What was the Selden Patent?

George Baldwin Selden was a patent lawyer who, after seeing a demonstration of the Brayton 2-cycle, internal combustion engine, decided to acquire a patent using it in a road vehicle. The patent was applied for in 1879 and granted sixteen years later.

How did the Selden Patent affect the North American auto industry?

Selden sold the patent rights to the Electric Vehicle Company which then successfully demanded royalties from all existing manufacturers. However, one group of manufacturers, led by Henry Ford, refused to buckle under. Defeated in the courts in 1909, Ford persisted and finally won in 1911. The court ruled that the Selden Patent only applied to 2-cycle engines of the Brayton principle.

Kansas farm boy Walter P. Chrysler served his apprenticeship with the Union Pacific Railroad and ultimately went on to found his own car company in 1924, largely financed by savings from his previous job. What was his previous job?

He was president of the Buick Division of General Motors, with a salary of $1,000,000 a year. Selling his GM stock for some $10 million also helped!

Walter P. Chrysler putting his seal of approval on one of the first cars bearing his name.

AUTOMANIA

Following WWII this European company was struggling to get into production. Offered in turn to the British auto industry and to Henry Ford II, it was dismissed by both. Sir William Rootes wouldn't take it even as a gift and Ford's advisor said the car was "no damn good". What was the company in question?
Volkswagen.

After nineteen years in production, what model replaced the Ford Model T?
The Model A, introduced in 1927 (1928 model).

When Henry Ford died, what three things were found in his pocket?
A pocketknife, a comb and a jew's-harp.

True or false: Gottleib Daimler and Karl Benz worked and lived only sixty miles apart and their two companies joined in 1926, but they never met.
True.

In 1903 John and Horace Dodge agreed to supply engines and running gear exclusively to another manufacturer. Who was it?
Henry Ford.

The Dodges were also investors in Ford. When they decided to discontinue supplying Ford and start their own company in 1914, they were able to finance it largely from earned dividends on their Ford stock. How much had their $10,000 investment earned them in eleven years: $1 million, $3.4 million or $5 million?
$5 million.

THE PIONEERS & OTHER BEGINNINGS

In 1919 Henry Ford decided not to issue any more dividends. What was the outcome?
The Dodge brothers sued, and won another $2 million.

That was it for Henry. He decided to buy out all the private stockholders and have complete control of his own company. How much did the Dodge brothers get for their $10,000 investment: $12 million, $18 million or $25 million?
$25 million.

How much did it cost Henry Ford to buy out all the private shareholders: $74 million, $106 million, or $187 million?
$106 million ($105.8 million exactly).

Before the Hon. Charles S. Rolls met Frederick H. Royce, he was already in the business as an agent in London for several European makes. Can you name them?
Panhard, Minerva and Mors.

Charles Rolls did not live to see the great success of the Rolls-Royce marque. He died in 1910, just five years after the birth of the company, at the age of thirty-three. What were the unusual circumstances of his death?
He was Britain's first aviation fatality. He crashed his Wright biplane while competing in an event at Bournemouth, England.

On January 10, 1886, the first patent for an automobile was granted to Karl Benz (with mustache at right), of Mannheim, Germany, for his three-wheeled car. Gottleib Daimler (with beard at left), working only sixty miles away in Cannstatt, built the first four-wheeled car a few months later.

Lionel Martin called his first car the Martin Aston. Subsequently, in partnership with R. Bamford, it became the Bamford and Martin Aston. Where did the Aston name come from?
From the Aston Clinton Hillclimb, where they used to compete.

Under new management in 1926 it became, simply, Aston Martin and, in 1947, passed into the hands of an English tractor company. What was the name of the new owner?
David Brown.

In the same year, David Brown took over another prestigious British make famous for high quality and high performance. What was it?
Lagonda.

American Wilbur Gunn grew up in Ohio and served his apprenticeship with the family company, the Singer Sheep Shearing Co. Inc. He moved to England to pursue a career as an opera singer but ended up building Lagonda cars. Where does the name Lagonda come from?
It comes from Lagonda Creek, a tributary of the Mad River in Ohio, close to where Wilbur grew up.

The great engineer W.O. Bentley was responsible for the cars bearing his name. Started in 1919, the company ran into difficulties in the 1931 Depression and was taken over by what other British company?
Rolls-Royce.

In 1894 Elwood P. Haynes of Kokomo, Indiana, demonstrated a vehicle he had built with the help of Elmo and Edgar Apperson. He billed it as "America's

The Hon. Charles S. Rolls cutting a dashing figure at the wheel of a Silver Ghost prior to the start of the Empire City Race of 1906.

first gasoline-powered vehicle". Who challenged this claim?

The Duryea brothers, whose own vehicle had been unveiled two years previously. After many years of litigation, they finally had their claim upheld.

Initially, Gottleib Daimler was more interested in selling his engines than complete automobiles. Name the two French companies that used Daimler engines.

Panhard & Levassor, and Peugeot.

How did Panhard & Levassor come to hold the Daimler license?

The rights for France had originally been purchased in 1887 by Edouard Sarazin. However, he died not long after and Emile Levassor married his widow, Louise, and set up Panhard & Levassor.

Who purchased the Daimler rights in England?

Frederick R. Simms, who formed the Daimler Motor Syndicate in 1890 and subsequently sold out to H.J. Lawson — the British "Selden" — who re-structured it as the Daimler Motor Company. Success was assured when Edward VII made Daimler the "royal" car in 1900.

Who purchased the Daimler rights in the United States?

The Steinway Piano Company of New York.

Cadillac was bought by General Motors in 1909 but remained in the control of founder Henry Leland. WWI caused a breach between Leland and GM President William Durant, resulting in Leland's resignation. What was the argument?

Leland wanted GM to mobilize for war production. Durant refused.

A classic "boat tail", 4-1/2 Litre Bentley.

AUTOMANIA

Leland then founded a new car company to compete with his own creation, Cadillac. What was the new company?
Lincoln.

Leland also threw himself into war work and joined the team that developed the most famous American aero engine of WWI. What was it called?
The Liberty engine.

The Lincoln car was a worthy competitor for Cadillac, but the company fell on bad times following the 1921-22 Depression. Leland had to sell out. Who was the buyer?
None other than Henry Ford, whom Leland had ousted from the Henry Ford Company back in 1902!

How much did Henry Ford pay for Lincoln?
A paltry $8 million. Within two years, Henry Leland was gone, resigning over differences with Henry Ford.

When did the Daimler and Benz companies merge: 1908, 1912 or 1926?
1926.

When they merged, they also combined their logos: a three-pointed star and a laurel wreath. Who provided what?
The three-pointed star came from Daimler, the laurel wreath from Benz.

What was the significance of the three-pointed star?
It indicated that Daimler provided engines for three uses: cars, boats and aircraft.

Proving a point. The power of this 1903 Model "A" Cadillac is demonstrated as, fully laden, it pulls a loaded wagon up Shelby St. Hill, Detroit. Al Brush is the driver.

Match these famous brothers to their surnames:

Louis, Gaston, Arthur	Duesenberg
Fred, August	Duryea
Frank, Charles	Dodge
John, Horace	Chevrolet

From the top: Chevrolet, Duesenberg, Duryea and Dodge

Where did John DeLorean go to get financing for his car company in 1980?
The British Government.

How much did he get: £15 million, £25 million, or £40 million?
£40 million.

Where did he build his plant?
Belfast, Northern Ireland.

Name two unique features of the DeLorean car.
Unpainted finish and gull-wing doors.

What engine did the DeLorean use?
The Renault PRV V-6.

What brought about the downfall of John DeLorean?
His arrest on charges of smuggling cocaine in 1982. All charges were subsequently dropped, but DeLorean remained entangled in a web of civil lawsuits concerning his operations.

The 1964 Sunbeam Tiger (from Britain's Rootes Group) had a powerful North American V-8 engine. What was it and who supplied it?
A 4.3 litre Ford V-8 of 164 b.h.p.

Why was this an odd arrangement?
Because the Rootes Group had been taken over by Chrysler.

Daimler and Benz combined their logos as well as their companies in 1926.

AUTOMANIA

What company started out manufacturing clothes wringers in 1869, switched to automobiles in 1900 and finally became a brewery in 1934?
Peerless.

What beer did they make?
Carling's Ale.

Who designed the world-famous Ford script logo?
Childe Harold Wills, Henry Ford's metallurgist.

In 1919 Wills left Ford to start his own automotive company. What was the car he introduced in 1921?
The Wills Sainte Claire.

What was the significance of the name?

It was derived from Lake St. Clair, north of Detroit. He added the 'e's because he thought it was "classier".

The engine in the Wills Sainte Claire was a copy of a famous European V-8. Was it based on Hispano-Suiza, Bugatti or Rolls-Royce?
Hispano-Suiza.

Wills Sainte Claire folded in 1927 but Childe Harold Wills was able to get another job. Who hired him?
Chrysler hired him as chief metallurgist.

Match these famous brothers with their surnames:

Ray, Robert, Joseph	Jensen
Windsor, Rollin, Walter	Stanley
Richard, Allan	Graham
Francis, Freelan	White

Only the Mercedes 300SL survived its "gull-wing" doors. They didn't work for the DeLorean.

From the top: Graham, White, Jensen, and Stanley.

Henry Leland of Cadillac and Lincoln fame shared the same kind of training as Gottleib Daimler. To what trade were they apprenticed?
Both were apprenticed gunmakers.

In John F. Dodge and Horace E. Dodge, what do the middle initials stand for?
Francis and Elgin.

What is Walter P. Chrysler's middle name?
Percy.

Walter Chrysler was succeeded by K.T. Keller, who assumed the presidency in 1940. What do the initials "K.T." stand for?
Kaufman Thuma.

In 1938 Adolf Hitler awarded this man the Grand Cross of the Supreme Order of the German Eagle for "making motor cars available to the masses". Who was the recipient: Louis Renault, Ferdinand Porsche or Henry Ford?
Henry Ford, who accepted it happily, without realizing the damaging effect it was to have on North American sales.

Swiss-born Louis Chevrolet emigrated to Canada in 1900 with brothers Arthur and Gaston. He first made his mark as a racing driver for this company. Was it Buick, Ford or Packard?
Buick.

Suitably attired for the Glidden Tour, this foursome looks like they're "having fun now" in their 1906 Peerless.

AUTOMANIA

He was approached by William Durant who was about to make a come-back after being deposed at General Motors. Together they launched the Chevrolet car in 1911. Chevrolet was to become the world's biggest-selling nameplate and a massive moneymaker. But not for Louis, who left after a disagreement with Durant and formed his own company. What was the company Louis Chevrolet formed?
Frontenac. Only moderately successful, the company folded in 1922. Louis never benefited from the success of Chevrolet and died in 1942, poor, sick and in virtual obscurity.

Why is the SCCA (Sports Car Club of America) happy every time another Firebird Trans Am is sold?

Because it's another five bucks in the kitty. The SCCA own rights to the term "Trans Am", a race series which they sanctioned. The royalty was arranged with General Motors for the use of the name.

In the 1979 "bail-out", how much money did the U.S. Government loan to Chrysler: was it $850 million, $1.5 billion, or $3.5 billion?
Not a penny! The U.S. Government merely agreed to "guarantee" loans of up to $1.5 billion. Chrysler borrowed from conventional sources and secured many concessions from suppliers and employees.

When did Chrysler pay off its loans: 1981, 1983, or 1985?
In July, 1983, seven years ahead of the due date.

The first woman to be issued a taxi driver permit in Berlin — and probably, the world — is shown with her first "fares" in this 1909 Adler.

THE PIONEERS & OTHER BEGINNINGS

In 1989 both the NHTSA and the Canadian Department of Transport issued reports discounting a phenomenon known as "unintended acceleration". Which company was most happy with these reports?
Audi of America, whose cars had been accused of this design fault. Extensive research indicated the cause to be "driver error".

Joint ventures are becoming the "norm" in the global auto wars. Can you identify these "marriages"?

Ford   Mitsubishi
General Motors   Mazda
Chrysler   Suzuki

From the top: Mazda, Suzuki, and Mitsubishi.

What company logo was taken from a piece of wallpaper ripped off a French hotel room wall?
William Durant, founder of General Motors, liked the design on his hotel wall so he ripped it off and brought it home. It became the famous "bow-tie" logo of Chevrolet.

A farmer at heart, Henry Ford financed an experimental car in 1941 that had a non-metal body. What was the basic ingredient used?
A soybean derivative.

When did Datsun become Nissan in North America: 1981, 1983, or 1985?
1981.

Louis Chevrolet's Frontenac.

AUTOMANIA

On January 5th, 1914, this manufacturer announced that shifts would be reduced from nine hours to eight, and pay would be doubled to $5.00 an hour. Was it: Henry Leland, William Durant, or Henry Ford?
Henry Ford.

What specialist car-builder used a scorpion as his corporate emblem?
Abarth.

What company emblem depicts a viking ship: Plymouth, Volvo, or Rover?
Rover.

In 1926 Chrysler introduced a new model with a scalloped radiator and hood which looked suspiciously like a classic British model. The British company promptly sued.... Was it Rolls-Royce, Lagonda, or Vauxhall?
Vauxhall. They lost the suit.

One year after Oldsmobile, the second mass-produced vehicle in the world appeared. What was it?
The Rambler Model D.

CHAPTER 2 ♛ RACES, RECORDS & RALLIES

Many of the first automobile contests were nothing more than demonstration trials designed to show people that cars were reliable and practical. The results were not always convincing in those early days, much to the delight of the anti-motoring majority who saw these new contrivances as the Devil's work. In spite of the — sometimes violent — opposition, contests of speed and endurance proliferated, forcing technical development at a staggering rate. Speed came first, at the expense of stability. This, combined with the poor quality of the roads and total lack of crowd control, led to some terrible accidents.

The result was to force race organizers off the public roads and onto "closed circuits" where spectators could be controlled and see the event with some measure of safety. But the underlying motivation remained to beat the opposition with a faster, more reliable vehicle and sell more cars as a result. Contests, trials and demonstration runs of one kind or another were taking place as early as vehicles could be produced, however the first race recognized as such took place in 1895.

The course ran from: London to Brighton, Green Bay to Madison, Wisconsin, or Paris to Bordeaux?
Paris to Bordeaux.

What newspaper sponsored the event?
Le Petit Journal of Paris.

A 1895 Panhard & Levassor

AUTOMANIA

It was also the first event to be sanctioned by what organizing body?
The Automobile Club de France.

There were 46 entries; only 22 started, 11 made it to Bordeaux and only nine finished. Who won?
Emile Levassor on his Panhard & Levassor. In what was to become somewhat characteristic of all French races, the first car to finish was disqualified on the grounds it had only two seats. It was a German Benz Victoria.

In its nineteen years of production, how many Ford Model Ts were built over 10 million, over 13 million, or over 15 million?
The official number is 15,007,003.

True or false: this production record has never been surpassed.
False. One other company passed this milestone in 1972.

What company and what model was it?
The Volkswagen Beetle, which is still in production in Mexico. As of September 30, 1989, production had reached 20,757,968.

Scandal at the races. The Italian Government wanted to really "hype" this event and so they made it the subject of a lottery, "The Lottery of Millions". What was the event: the Italian Grand Prix, the Targa Florio, or the Tripoli Grand Prix?
The Tripoli Grand Prix of 1933.

Pisa timber merchant Enrico Rivio purchased a ticket with a leading driver's name. Was it Tazio Nuvolari,

Jochen Rindt in a familiar position — leading Hill, Clark and Amon.

Louis Chiron, or Achile Varzi?
Achille Varzi.

Enrico approached Varzi and promised to split the winnings — 8.5 million lira — if Varzi could "contrive" to win. Varzi had a pre-race meeting with Nuvolari, Campari, Borzacchini, and Chiron in order, it is alleged, to contrive just that. But something went wrong during the race. What was it?
Varzi lost two cylinders on his Bugatti very early on and was left miles behind his co-conspirators. The second half of the race became a kind of Keystone Cops comedy as Chiron, Campari, and the others tried to eliminate themselves with dignity and allow Varzi to win. Borzacchini drove into some oil drums at a corner; Chiron had "mechanical problems"; Campari simply went to the pits and never came out; Nuvolari, well in the lead, and running smoothly, became desperate as he looked in vain for Varzi in his mirrors and simply slowed down, finally stopping within sight of the finish line because he was "out of gas". He and his pit crew then did a slow motion re-fuelling that must have been painful to watch. And finally, Varzi came chugging by to cross the finish line to the jeers and boos of the crowd in the grandstand. Varzi was practically in a coma of nervous exhaustion and fear and had to be pried from the car. But he won.

What was the eventual outcome?
There were charges and accusations but no disciplinary action was taken. However, the next year, the numbers were not drawn until immediately prior to the race.

In 1901 this auto race between New York and Buffalo was stopped at Rochester upon learning of the assassination of the U.S. President. Which President was it?
President McKinley.

Beginning in 1928, Miller-engined cars were to enjoy remarkable success at Indianapolis. They won a total of 6, 9, or 11 '500's?
A total of nine, with seven consecutive wins between 1928 and 1934. Two additional wins came in '36 and '38.

In 1925 Miss Violet Corderey drove one of these British sports cars around the world in order to help sales. Was it a Bentley, a Straker-Squire, or an Invicta?
An Invicta.

She also set two remarkable records at the famous test track outside Paris. She ran 25,000 kms at an average of 55.7 mph, and 5,000 miles at 70.7 mph. What is the name of the test track?
Montlhery.

As a result, what prestigious trophy did she win for Invicta?
The Dewar Trophy.

What was "Le Pur Sang"?
Ettore Bugatti's first light racing car.

The first banked racing circuit in the world was completed in 1907. Where was it located: Paris, Weybridge, or Modena?
Brooklands at Weybridge in Surrey, England.

This vintage French racing driver served as chauffeur to Generals Petain and Foch during WW1. Who was he?
Louis Chiron.

AUTOMANIA

The first Glidden Tour attracted 77 starters, of whom only eleven did not finish. The route was from New York to the St. Louis Exposition and it took place in 1903, 1904, or 1905?
1904.

Only one race driver has ever won the World Driving Championship posthumously. Was it Count Wolfgang von Trips, Lorenzo Bandini, or Jochen Rindt?
Jochen Rindt in 1970. He was killed in practice for the Italian Grand Prix but had accumulated enough points to win the Championship.

Only one American-born race driver has ever won the World Driving Championship. Was it Dan Gurney, Phil Hill, or Mario Andretti?
Phil Hill in 1961. Mario Andretti was born in Italy and Dan Gurney never won the Championship.

Who was Phil Hill driving for?
Ferrari.

Only one Canadian has ever won on the Grand Prix circuit. Who was he?
Gilles Villeneuve.

How did he meet his death?
He was killed while practicing for the 1982 Belgian Grand Prix.

1910 Vanderbilt Cup: Mort Robert and riding mechanic Harry Nichen in their Abbott-Detroit. Falling off was a definite possibility.

How many Grand Prix did he win in his career?
A total of six.

What Grand Prix driver sported the colours of the London Rowing Club on his helmet?
Graham Hill.

The annual London to Brighton Emancipation Run was first staged in 1896 to celebrate: The Relief of Mafeking; Votes for Women; or the repeal of the 4 mph speed limit?
The repeal of the 4 mph speed limit and the need for vehicles to be preceded by a man carrying a red flag.

Juan Manuel Fangio won the World Driving Championship five times in four different marques: Maserati in '57; Ferrari in '56; Mercedes in '55; Maserati/Mercedes in '54; and...
Alfa Romeo in '51.

What racing driver always kept a spare, plastic right ear?
Frenchman Jean Behra lost his right ear in a 1955 accident and used a plastic replacement. Since he made a habit of crashing, he had to keep spares available.

The Mille Miglia road race was cancelled forever following a fatal accident to this driver in 1957. Was it Lorenzo Bandini, Count Wolfgang von Trips, or Alphonse de Portago?
Spanish nobleman Alphonse de Portago.

Phil Hill, the only American-born World Driving Champion.

What car was he driving?
A Ferrari.

Where did the accident occur?
Outside the village of Guidizollo—only about 30 miles from the finish.

How many people were killed?
Eleven, including Portago's riding navigator Gurner Nelson.

What position was he in when he crashed?
Third, and gaining on von Trips' Ferrari.

Who won the race?
Piero Taruffi, also in a Ferrari.

In 1955 this English driver, in a German car, set the all time speed record for the Mille Miglia. Was it Stirling Moss, Peter Collins, or Mike Hawthorn?
Stirling Moss.

Stirling's winning time had much to do with the thorough preparation of his riding navigator, who was...?
Journalist and ex-motorcycle racer, Denis Jenkinson.

What car was Stirling driving?
A Mercedes-Benz 300SLR.

Graham Hill never went this fast in the single sculls.

What was the significance of the number 722 on Stirling's winning Mercedes?
Numbers indicate the starting time of each vehicle. The Moss Mercedes left the start at 7:22 A.M.

Where did the Mille Miglia start and finish?
At Brescia.

Mille Miglia means "Thousand Miles". Why would an Italian race use this terminology instead of kilometres?

The "milles" are based on the old Roman "mile".

The first Indianapolis 500 race was staged in: 1908, 1911, or 1913?
1911.

The first race at Indianapolis Speedway did not involve cars. Was it a race for horses, balloons, or motorcycles?
Balloons, in June, 1908. The first car race took place two months later.

Tired but happy. Denis Jenkinson (1) and Stirling Moss at the finish of the 1955 Mille Miglia.

AUTOMANIA

Where would you go to see races at these venues: Montlhery, The Brickyard, and Monza?
Paris, Indianapolis, and Milan.

Why would ex-World Driving Champion Jackie Stewart have difficulty reading the words on this page?
He suffers from a form of dyslexia.

Only one race has ever been won by a car driving backwards over the finish line. What was the race and who won it?
The 1919 Targa Florio was won by Andre Boillot driving a 1914 Peugeot. Exhaustion caused him to lose control and spin off the course a few yards from the finish. Dazed, he got back on the course facing the wrong way and so reversed over the finish line.

What car won the first Indianapolis 500 in 1911? Was it a Mercedes, a National, or a Marmon? Clue: it was racing in its home town.
A Marmon Wasp. It took 6 hours, 42 minutes, and 8 seconds at an average speed of 74.602 mph.

Who was the winning driver?
Ray Harroun.

What was Ray Harroun's nickname?
The Bedouin.

What racing drivers were known by these nicknames: The Shunt, The Flying Mantuan, and The Mod Scot?
James Hunt, Tazio Nuvolari, and Jackie Stewart.

The rear-view mirror is prominent on this legendary Indy racer.

How did the "pits" in racing get that name?
Mechanics at the 1908 French Grand Prix in Dieppe dug pits beside the course in order to service the cars from underneath. The practice wasn't continued, but the name stuck.

This actor, with co-driver Peter Revson, finished second in the 1970 12 Hours of Sebring. Was it Paul Newman, James Garner, or Steve McQueen?
Steve McQueen.

Who was the first Briton to win the Indianapolis 500? Clue: he was already the World Driving Champion.
Jim Clark in 1965.

What British World Driving Champion always went racing wearing a bow tie?
Mike Hawthorn.

How did Italian champion Alberto Ascari get soaked at Monte Carlo in 1955?
Not at the casino. He drove into the harbor during the Monaco Grand Prix.

It didn't exactly start a trend but one other driver did the same thing ten years later. Who was it?
Briton Paul Hawkins, driving a Lotus-Climax.

In 1903 Count Eliot Zborowski, driving a Mercedes at the La Turbie Hillclimb in Nice, crashed fatally when his cuff-links caught in the hand throttle causing the vehicle to accelerate into the cliffside. Twenty-two years later his son, Count Louis Zborowski, was also killed racing. There was a bizarre link between the two deaths. What was it?
Louis was also driving a Mercedes, during the Italian Grand Prix. But stranger still, he was wearing the same cuff-links that caused his father's death.

The modern World Driver's Championship began in 1950. Who was the first winner: Juan Fangio, Alberto Ascari, or Guiseppe Farina?
Dr. Guiseppe Farina, driving for Alfa Romeo.

Farina is credited with introducing a particular style of driving to the Grand Prix circuits. What is it?
Farina drove sitting well back with outstretched arms. This was quite different from the previous "wheel in the chest and bent elbows school". The new "relaxed" style was quickly adopted by other drivers like Stirling Moss.

Who was the first American to win a Grand Prix race? Clue: he won the Indianapolis 500 the following year.
Jimmy Murphy won the 1921 French Grand Prix at Dieppe.

What car was he driving? Was it a Duesenberg, a Mercedes, or a Fiat?
A Duesenberg.

The following year he took the same car to Indianapolis and won the 500; but there was a major difference to the car. What was it?
Much to the disgust of Fred and Augie Duesenberg, Murphy replaced their engine with a new Miller powerplant.

Canada's first-ever Formula One Grand Prix took place at Mosport in 1967. Who was the winner: Gilles Villeneuve, Jim Clark, or Jack Brabham?
Jack Brabham in a Repco-Brabham V-8.

AUTOMANIA

On January 12, 1904, a race car called "Arrow" set a new speed record for the mile, at 91.37 mph. The attempt took place on the frozen surface of Lake St. Clair, Michigan. Who was the driver: Barney Oldfield, William K. Vanderbilt, or Henry Ford?
Henry Ford. Naturally, the mark was not accepted by the Automobile Club de France and so it remains "unofficial".

What race driver sported a checkerboard design on his helmet?
Innes Ireland (also Jean Behra).

What was the first rear-engined car to race at the Indianapolis 500? Was it a Copper-Climax, a Miller-Gulf, or an Auto-Union?
The Miller-Gulf raced in the 1939 event but dropped out after 47 laps. Incidentally, it also featured 4WD.

Germany's Auto-Union racing cars of the thirties broke with engineering tradition by placing the engine behind the driver. However, this wasn't so new. What other German company had previously developed a rear-engined race car?
The Benz Tropfenwagen of 1923 had a rear-engine and quite advanced aerodynamic styling.

Who designed the racing Auto-Unions?
Ferdinand Porsche.

In 1964, A.J. Foyt, Jr., won his second Indianapolis 500 driving the Sheraton-Thompson Special. What was

1922 Indy Winner Jimmy Murphy in his Duesenberg ' "Murphy Special".

significant about this win?
*It was the last time a front-engine racer
would take the checkered flag at Indy!*

The early races featured long-distance,
city-to-city events combining high
speed and endurance. However, these
events were brought to an end by a
disastrous race staged in 1903. The
course was: Paris to Vienna, Paris to
Amsterdam, or Paris to Madrid?
Paris to Madrid.

An early fatality was one of the
Renault brothers. Was it Marcel, Louis,
or Fernand?
Marcel.

In the first section of the race there
were scores of accidents that left two
drivers, three mechanics and several
spectators killed or injured. The race
was aborted at Chateaudun, Bordeaux,
or Poitiers?
Bordeaux.

The first American trans-continental
race took place in 1901, 1905, or
1907?
1905.

Only two cars, provided by the same
company, took part. What were they?
They were both Curved Dash Oldsmobiles.

What were the nicknames of the cars?
"Old Steady" and "Old Scout".

The route ran from New York to: San
Francisco, Seattle or Portland?
Portland.

Innes Ireland was always one of
the most intense GP drivers.

August 5th, 1905. Henry Ford, with goggles, is about to attempt (unsuccessfully) to lower the World Land Speed Record
in his Model K Racer.

AUTOMANIA

Which car won?
"Old Scout", driven by Dwight Huss and Milford Wigle.

How long had the crossing taken: 42 days, 44 days, or 68 days?
44 days to cover the 3,890 mile journey. "Old Steady", driven by Percy Megargel and Barton Stanchfield, arrived four days later.

Why was the Le Mans winning Ford designated "GT 40"?
Because it stood 40" high.

What year did the Ford GT40 win the Le Mans 24-Hour classic?

1968 and 1969. A Ford Mk. IIA won in 1966 and a Mk. IV in 1967.

That most Italian of all road races, the Targa Florio, has only been won twice by British drivers, in 1912 and 1955. The first winner was Cyril Snipe of Manchester who was sent to Italy to supervise shipment of S.C.A.T. cars to England. He won at the wheel of a S.C.A.T. Who was the second Briton to win? Clue: he would win the Mille Miglia in the same year.
Stirling Moss.

A racing Renault of 1904.

The 1922 Benz "Tropfenwagen" sports-racer taking part in a 1930 parade in Berlin.

What was Stirling driving?
A Mercedes-Benz 300SLR.

He was accompanied by a co-driver who would lose his life three years later at Nurburgring. Who was he?
Peter Collins.

At the 1952 24-Hours of Le Mans, one driver attempted to run the whole race single-handed. Who was it?
Pierre Levegh.

How did his race end?
With only 75 minutes to go, and many miles in the lead, he collapsed from exhaustion and did not finish!

Three years later he returned to Le Mans and was given a car by what factory? Was it a Mercedes, a Talbot, or a Jaguar?
A Mercedes.

In this race, Levegh was involved in an accident that cost him his life and killed 83 spectators when a car swerved in front of him on the pit straight, causing his car to climb up its back and become airborne. What was the car that swerved in front of him?
An Austin-Healey driven by Lance Macklin.

What was he driving?
A Talbot which he had prepared personally.

A.J. Foyt in the last of a kind.

Why did Macklin swerve?
To avoid hitting Mike Hawthorn who was pulling over into the pits.

Who eventually won the race?
Mike Hawthorn. The leading Mercedes' were withdrawn when far in the lead, leaving Hawthorn to win.

What car was Hawthorn driving?
A D-Type Jaguar.

Where is (was) the Targa Florio race held?
On the island of Sicily.

During practise for the 1906 Targa Florio, racers complained of an unusual hazard in the mountains. What was it?
They were being shot at by bandits.

How did race organizer Count Florio handle the situation?
He hired the top three bandits in the area and made them Stewards of the Course — a system that was employed successfully thereafter.

In 1907 one of the great road races of all time took place. The course ran from Peking to what European capital: Berlin, Paris, or London?
Paris.

Five vehicles took part: two French De Dions, one Contal 3-wheeler, one Dutch Spyker, and an Itala. Which vehicle won?
The Itala.

It looks as if they've just completed their historic trans-continental drive.

RACES, RECORDS & RALLIES

Who officially drove the Itala?
Prince Scipio Borghese.

Who did most of actual the driving?
The family chauffeur, Ettore Guizzardi (who else?).

The race was sponsored by what French newspaper?
Le Matin.

What is a "Le Mans start"?
Where the drivers line up, on the far side of the circuit, opposite their cars, and have to sprint across the track at the drop of the flag.

When was the first World Land Speed Record set: 1898, 1900, or 1903?

1898. It was set by Count Gaston Chasscloup-Laubat in a 40h.p. Jenteaud Electric, on the Archeres Road, outside Paris.

What was the blistering speed that the count established: 28.75 mph, 39.24 mph, or 43.64 mph?
39.24 mph.

In 1906, at Ormond Beach, Florida, this steam car surprised the world with a record run of 121.57 mph. What was the car?
The Stanley Rocket.

This 1955 Mercedes 300 SLR shows some wear and tear in the Targa Florio. Who is driving?
Peter Collins. His co-driver was Stirling Moss — they won.

AUTOMANIA

Who drove it?

Fred Marriott. In the following year, Marriott narrowly survived a crash when attempting a new record. The accident so upset the Stanley brothers that they withdrew from all competition.

During the twenties and thirties, the World Land Speed Record was pretty well owned by cars from what country: the United States, France, or Great Britain?

Great Britain.

Match these famous British record holders with their equally famous cars:

Sir Malcolm Campbell	"Babs"
George Eyston	"Golden Arrow"
Sir Henry de Hane	"Thunderbolt"
Segrave	"Bluebird"
Parry Thomas	

From the top: "Bluebird", "Thunderbolt", "Golden Arrow", and "Babs".

Only once has the World Land Speed Record been set in the Southern Hemisphere. It was set by the son of a previous British WLSR holder. Who was it?

Donald Campbell, son of Sir Malcolm Campbell.

The De Dion Bouton that took part in the incredible Peking to Paris Race. On display probably at the Paris Auto Salon in 1909.

RACES, RECORDS & RALLIES

Where did the record attempt take place?
Lake Eyre, Australia.

What speed was accomplished: 398.70 mph; 403.10 mph or 411.63 mph?
403.10 mph

Donald Campbell, Henry Segrave and John Cobb were all WLSR holders. What else do they have in common?
They were all killed attempting to break the World Water Speed Record.

Parry Thomas was killed in "Babs" during a 1927 attempt on the WLSR. Where was the attempt held?
Pendine Sands, Wales.

The WLSR for vehicles with "driven" wheels — as opposed to jet-powered vehicles — was set in 1965 by an American team, with a speed of 409.277 mph. What was the name of the vehicle?
"Goldenrod".

Who drove it?
Bob Summers.

Ormond Beach, Florida saw many record runs. This effort by Fred Marriott in 1906 surprised the "gasoline-engine" crowd.

Le Mans start, 1953 version. Note the circles painted on the other side of the road. The drivers must stand there until the flag drops.

AUTOMANIA

What engines were used?
Four Chrysler, 426 CID, V-8, Hemis in line.

The fastest speed recorded (to date) was established by a British team in 1983, with a clocking of 634.052 mph. What was the name of the vehicle?
"Thrust II".

What power source was used?
A Rolls-Royce Avon jet engine.

The oldest race driver to win a Grand Prix did so in 1951 at the French GP. Was it Piero Taruffi, Luigi Fagioli, or Louis Chiron?
Luigi Fagioli. He was 53.

Only one World Driving Champion was also a World Motorcycle Champion.

Was it Tazio Nuvolari, John Surtees, or Nicki Lauda?
John Surtees was World Motorcycle Champion eight times before turning his attention to race cars.

Surtees won the World Driving Championship in 1964. What team was he driving for?
Ferrari.

True or false: points earned at the Indianapolis 500 count in the World Driver's Championship?
False. They only counted until 1960.

Match these famous dragsters with their nicknames:
Don Garlits   "The Mongoose"
Bill Jenkins   "The Snake"

Sir Malcolm Campbell at Daytona Beach, after setting a record of 245.733 mph. What's the name of his car?
The Bluebird.

RACES, RECORDS & RALLIES

Don Prudhomme   "Big Daddy"
Tom McEwan   "Grumpy"
From the top: "Big Daddy", "Grumpy",
"The Snake", and "The Mongoose".

What was the name of the private
Scottish team that won the Le Mans
24-Hour Race for Jaguar in 1956?
Ecurie Ecosse.

Who were the drivers?
Ron Flockhart and Ninian Sanderson.

What were the "Lance-Corporal",
"Corporal", and "Sergeant"?
Ecurie Ecosse painted horizontal stripes on
the nose of each D-Type Jaguar to make
them easily identifiable for the pit crew: one
stripe for "Lance-Corporal", two for
"Corporal" and three for "Sergeant".

What clothing manufacturer currently
(1989) sponsors a Formula One racing
team?
Benetton sponsors the Benetton-Ford team.

The fastest with driven wheels.

Ex-motorcycle champion,
John Surtees.

AUTOMANIA

Juan Fangio won the 1956 World Championship in unusual circumstances when a teammate who was leading in the standings handed over his vehicle. Who was this driver?
Peter Collins.

Why did Collins hand over his car?
Collins enjoyed being a race driver but, at age 25, he felt unprepared for the celebrity status and the responsibilities he would have to face as "world champion".

What was the first British car to win the Formula One Constructor's Championship?
Vanwall, in 1958.

This company brought turbo-charging back to Formula One racing in 1977.

Was it Ford, Lotus, or Renault?
Renault.

Which Formula One team campaigned six-wheeled racers in 1976?
Tyrrell.

The first trans-America crossing by car took place in 1903. Dr. H. Nelson Jackson drove a second-hand Winton from San Francisco to New York. How long did it take: 64 days, 72 days, or 79 days?
64 days. On his way home from New York to Burlington, Dr. Jackson got a ticket for exceeding the 6 mph speed limit!

When did the first trans-Canada crossing by car take place: 1904, 1908, or 1912?
1912.

The "lance-corporal" at speed. Ivor Bueb in the winning D-Type at Le Mans, 1957.

Thomas Wilby and F.V. Haney drove a Reo from Halifax to Vancouver. How long did it take: 64 days, 67 days, or 73 days?
67 days.

What was the purpose of the trip?
To publicize the Reo car and to draw attention to the need for a trans-Canada highway.

Ab Jenkins was a famous record setter in the twenties with his car, "The Mormon Meteor". What was Jenkins' other job?
He was mayor of Salt Lake City.

The Indianapolis Motor Speedway was conceived by this man in 1908. He was also co-owner of Prest-O-Lite. Who was he?
Carl Fisher.

The Speedway almost died after the first racing program. The tar and gravel track broke up under the terrific pounding and resulted in numerous accidents. What happened as a result?
The circuit was paved with bricks.

As a result, the Speedway became known by what nickname?
The Brickyard.

How many bricks did it take to pave the circuit: 1.2 million, 2.9 million, or 3.2 million?
3.2 million.

Turbocharging gave Renault's 1500 cc, V-6 engine over 500 h.p. at 11,000 rpm!

How much prize money was offered at the first Indianapolis 500?
$25,000, with $10,000 of it going to the winner.

What is the name of the trophy which is awarded to the Indianapolis 500 winner?
The Borg-Warner Trophy.

What is the unique feature of this trophy?
Each winner has his portrait added to the trophy in the form of a miniature sculpture.

The Indianapolis 500 takes credit for the introduction of the rear-view mirror. What vehicle first used it there?
The winning Marmon in the first "500" of 1911.

Why did this particular racer install a rear-view mirror?
Virtually all race cars of that period were two-seaters and required the use of a "riding mechanic". Part of his job was to keep the driver informed of what was happening behind. However, the winning Marmon Wasp was a single-seater and so driver Ray Harroun came up with the rear-view mirror idea.

What was the first foreign car to win the Indianapolis 500: Mercedes, Napier, or Peugeot?
A Peugeot in 1913.

What did the winning driver, Jules Goux, do in 1913 that would get him disqualified today?
He quaffed champagne during pit stops.

Jackson and Crocker in their second-hand Winton. Note "Bud" the bulldog sitting in front of Jackson. "Bud attached himself to the expedition in Caldwell, Idaho.

The Chevrolet brothers were successful at Indy in 1920 in a race car of their own design. What was it?
A Monroe.

With further success the following year in their Chevrolet-designed Frontenacs, they were approached by what manufacturer to assist race car development?
None other than Henry Ford.

The vehicles they developed were a combination of Ford and Frontenac engineering. What were the cars called?
Fronty-Fords.

The first two-time Indy winner took the checkered flag in a Frontenac (1921)

and a Miller Special (1923). Who was it?
Tommy Milton.

The first FWD race car appeared at Indy in 1925 and came second, driven by Dave Lewis. The FWD system would later be used on the Cord. What was the car?
The Miller.

The first "pace-car" at the Indy 500 in 1911 was a Packard, a Stutz, or a Stoddard-Dayton?
A Stoddard-Dayton.

Pit stops have never been the same since this 1913 winner.

AUTOMANIA

The Indy "pace-car" is usually driven by someone directly related to the race or an ex-winner. However, on three occasions it was driven by the movie star who did his own driving in the movie Grand Prix. Who is he?
James Garner drove a Buick in 1975, an Olds Delta 88 in 1977 and an Olds Calais in 1985.

When the winner of the Indy 500 gets to the Winner's Circle, what is he given to drink?
Milk.

In the early twenties, Carl Fisher lost interest in the Motor Speedway and sold his share. The new manager was a WWI American flying ace who had also been chauffeur to General Jack Pershing. Who was he?
Eddie Rickenbacker.

Rickenbacker made a number of improvements to the Motor Speedway, but one of the great traditions began to disappear. What was it?
The brick surface. Higher speeds had proved too much for the brick surface on the banked turns. These areas were asphalted, leaving bricks only on the two long straights.

In 1936 Louis Meyer became the first racer at Indy to do this. What was it?
He became the first man to win the Indy 500 three times. His previous wins were in 1932 and 1934.

A.J. Foyt, Jr. is one of the two drivers who have won the Indy 500 four times. Who is the other?
Al Unser.

1921 Indy winner Tommy Milton at the wheel of the Chevrolet-designed Frontenac. That's Barney Oldfield with the cigar and Louis Chevrolet in the homburg and moustache.

RACES, RECORDS & RALLIES

World Champion Jack Brabham was practically laughed off the Speedway when he showed up in 1961. Why?
He was driving a "funny", rear-engined Formula One Cooper-Climax.

How did he finish?
In ninth position. In the process, he demonstrated that the end was in sight for front-engined racers.

The first rear-engined car to win the Indy 500 was: a Cooper-Climax, an American Eagle, or a Lotus-Ford?
Lotus-Ford.

Who was the driver: Graham Hill, Jim Clark, or Jackie Stewart?
Jim Clark.

At the 1963 Indy 500 post-race

luncheon, why did Parnelli Jones punch Eddie Sachs in the mouth?
Parnelli Jones won the race but was dropping oil for the last 50 miles. Eddie Sachs was lying fourth when he spun off as a result of the oil. The post-race argument led to the punch.

Jim Clark's Indy 500 win was the first by a foreigner since Dario Resta in 1916. What car did Dario Resta drive: Delage, Peugeot, or Mercedes?
Peugeot.

Over the years, the bricks at The Brickyard have been replaced by modern paving. How many bricks actually remain?
All that remain are a symbolic eight rows at the start-finish line.

The first three-time Indy Champion.

AUTOMANIA

The Indy 500 has only twice been won by two drivers sharing the winning car. In what years did this occur?
1924 and 1941.

In 1941 Floyd Davis shared the ride with Mauri Rose, Wilbur Shaw, or Louis Meyer?
Mauri Rose.

In 1924 Len Coram and Joe Boyer brought home the winning car. Coram received the full prize of $20,000. What did Joe Boyer get?
$50 for leading the first lap!

In 1946 the Indianapolis Speedway came under new ownership, headed by Wilbur Shaw and Tony Hulman. What is Tony Hulman's first name?
Anton.

No woman has ever qualified to race at the Indy 500. But one came close in 1976. Who was it?
Janet Guthrie.

The first official road race in North America took place on Thanksgiving Day of 1895, 1897, or 1899?
1895.

Sponsored by the Chicago Times-Herald, the original course ran from Chicago to Waukegan, but the severe winter weather resulted in a much-shortened route of some 54 miles. Of the six starters, only a Duryea and a Benz finished. Who won?
The American Duryea. However, both cars were subsequently disqualified and the $300 in prize money was shared between all the contestants.

Scottish sheep farmer Jim Clark, "The Flying Scotsman".

RACES, RECORDS & RALLIES

The greatest race of all time took place in 1908. It was a Round-the-World Challenge. The starting point was Times Square, New York. Where was the finish to be: London, Paris, or Berlin?
Paris.

The race was sponsored by three newspapers: Paris' Le Matin, The Chicago Tribune, and...
The New York Times.

Six cars lined up for the start on February 12, 1908. They were a De Dion, Motobloc and Sizaire-Naudin from France; a Brixia-Zust from Italy; a Protos from Germany; and a Thomas Flyer from the U.S. What was the first car to reach Paris?
The German Protos on July 26, 1908.

What happened when the Protos crew claimed victory?
It was promptly disqualified by the French for "freighting" the car over the Rockies and bypassing Japan altogether.

Chicago, November 28, 1895: Frank Duryea at the tiller of the winning car in America's first race. Beside him is A.W. White, an umpire, from Toronto, Ontario.

Times Square, New York City, February 12, 1908: the Brixia-Zust (l) and the German Protos about to start on the Great New York to Paris Race.

Who won the race?
The American Thomas Flyer which arrived in Paris four days later. After an incredible five and a half month adventure, the crew of Charles Schuster, Hans Hansen, George Miller and George McAdam had prevailed.

The Brixia-Zust was awarded second prize when it finally reached Paris, but they had been held up by unusual circumstances in Russia, where they were briefly imprisoned as spies. Why?
They had tried to send a long cable from Omsk to their sponsor in Italy. The authorities had to be convinced that the message was not in secret code, just Italian!

American Motors was not noted for either high performance cars or great racing successes. But it did enjoy a moment of glory in 1971 and 1972 when it won this prestigious series. Was it the NASCAR Championship, the Trans-Am Championship, or the Can-Am Championship?
The Trans-Am Championship.

A closer look at the Italian Brixia-Zust team shortly after the start of the race. Note the chains on the rear wheels.

The ultimate winner of the New York to Paris race. The Thomas Flyer is seen leaving the city. All contestants later agreed that the most atrocious conditions on the whole route were those in the state of New York.

RACES, RECORDS & RALLIES

What car did AMC campaign in this series: a Hurst-Scrambler, a Javelin AMX, or a Hornet SC-360?
Javelin AMX.

Who prepared the car and managed the 1972 race program for AMC?
Roy Woods.

Who was the successful driver?
George Follmer.

This famous German race-driver was killed during a World Speed Record attempt on the Frankfurt-Darmstadt Autobahn in 1938. Who was he?
Bernd Rosemeyer.

Before racing became so commercial, race cars were painted in national colour schemes. Match these colours to the country:

Silver (originally white)   Great Britain
Yellow   U.S.A.
White with blue stripes   Germany
Green   Belgium

From the top: Germany, Belgium, U.S.A., Great Britain.

Bernd Rosemeyer (shown here at the 1937 German GP at the Nurburgring) and Tazio Nuvolari, were the only two drivers to really "handle" the rear-engined Auto-Unions.

A pit stop during the 1971 Trans Am series. The first win for American Motors, with Mark Donohue at the wheel and the Roger Penske crew.

Here are some more national racing colours to match with countries:

Blue   Holland
Red   France
Orange   Italy

From the top: France, Italy, Holland.

It gets harder — match these racing colours to their countries:

Pale violet   Canada
Blue, yellow and black   Egypt
Red with a white stripe   Argentina

From the top: Egypt, Argentina, Canada.

And harder:

Blue with silver stripe   Ireland
White with blue Latin   Austria
    cross   Finland
Green with orange band

From the top: Austria, Finland, Ireland.

Only four race drivers have (so far) won the World Driver's Championship and the Indianapolis 500. Can you name them?
Jim Clark, Graham Hill, Mario Andretti and Emmerson Fittipaldi.

What do these flag signals mean at the race circuit?
Yellow with vertical red stripes
Blue (motionless)
White
From the top: oil on the track; you are being followed closely; ambulance is on the circuit.

And what about these flags?
Red
Yellow (waved)
Black and white chequered

Briggs Cunningham (left), working on cars that finished 3rd, 7th, and 10th, in the 1953 Le Mans classic.

From the top: complete and immediate stop; great danger, prepare to stop; signal to winner and end of race.

What event would you be watching at "The Rest and be Thankful"?
The famous Scottish Hill Climb event.

What was the "Thinwall Special"?
A 4-1/2 litre Ferrari campaigned by Tony Vandervell of Vandervell Bearings and used as a "test bed" for their own car.

The race car that developed from the "Thinwall Special" was the first British car to win the Formula 1 Constructors' Championship. What was the car called?
The Vanwall.

What year did it win the Championship?
1958.

Who is the "odd man out": Phil Hill, Jackie Stewart or Stirling Moss?
Stewart and Hill are both ex-World Driving Champions; Moss never won the title.

This American did much to further the U.S. cause in international racing, including the development of an American sports car and a third place finish in the 1959 Le Mans race. His middle name is Swift. Who is he?
Briggs Cunningham.

Kenelm Lee Guinness, famous thirties British racer, also gave his name to a well-known automotive component. What is it?
KLG Spark Plugs.

Who is the fastest woman on wheels?
Kitty O'Neil.

In 1976 she drove the SMI Motivator to a speed of 439 mph, 524 mph, or 579 mph?
524 mph.

In 1975 Lella Lombardi did something at the Spanish Grand Prix that no other woman has, so far, equalled. What was it?
She won points in the Formula 1 Championship. At least, she won 1/2 a point by finishing in sixth place when the race was stopped following an accident.

In 1980 Canadians Gary Sowerby and Ken Langley beat Phileas Fogg's record. What was it?
The circumnavigation of the world.

Phileas Fogg did it in 80 days (fictionally, of course). How long did it take Sowerby and Langley?
77 days.

What vehicle did they use?
A Volvo 245 wagon.

What is ex-World Driving Champion Jackie Y. Stewart's middle name?
Young.

CHAPTER 3 ☆ THE CAR IN ENTERTAINMENT

What do you do after you've thrown several hundred cream pies, clung to the edge of a few skyscrapers and been tied to the railroad tracks a dozen times? That was the problem facing early moviemakers like Hal Roach. Fortunately for him and his confreres, a man named Henry Ford had launched a social revolution with his Model T, a vehicle within the financial reach of the masses, an audience that the early moviemakers were serving as well. It was a perfect match. The Model T was not a rich man's toy, as were so many of the early makes. It was cheap, it was fun and it even looked comical.

From the wonderful "collapsing" Model Ts of Laurel and Hardy, to the sophisticated gadgetry of James Bond, the automobile continues to play an exciting role in every form of entertainment.

It all started with Hal Roach and a crazy crew of "silent" minions of the law. What were they called?
The Keystone Cops.

What was the preferred mode of transport in the Hal Roach comedies?
Model T Fords.

The car used by Mrs. Emma Peel in the British TV series, "The Avengers" was: an MG, a Morgan, or a Lotus Elan?
A Lotus Elan.

Typical of the early use of cars in movies: Lawrence Semon of Vitagraph, accompanied by Joe Simburg and Earle Montgomery, leaping a mighty chasm in pursuit of "thrills and spills".

AUTOMANIA

And what car did John Steed drive in the same series: a Jaguar, a Bentley, or an Aston Martin?
A 4-1/2 litre Bentley.

In what car did Robert De Niro and his pals go hunting in the movie *The Deer Hunter?* Was it a 1959 Cadillac, a 1960 Chrysler Imperial, or a 1962 Lincoln?
A 1959 Cadillac.

In the George Burns movie *Oh God*, it rained inside this car. Was it a Chevrolet Vega, an AMC Pacer, or a Ford Thunderbird?
An AMC Pacer.

In the 1978 movie *Superman*, Lois Lane is nearly buried alive in this car. Was it a Ford Torino, Chevrolet Nova, or VW Beetle?
A 1972 Ford Torino.

In the Chevy Chase movie *Vacation*, a Ford station wagon is disguised and given a fictitious name. What was it called?
The Wagon Queen Family Truckster.

What car did Michael J. Fox use to go *Back to the Future*? Was it a Pantera, an Avanti, or a DeLorean?
A DeLorean.

This movie, starring Dick Van Dyke and Sally Ann Howes, told the story of a magical car that could fly and float. What was the movie?
Chitty-Chitty-Bang-Bang.

In the book of the same name, "Chitty-Chitty-Bang-Bang" had a previous existence under another name. What was it previously known as?
"The Paragon Panther".

It started out as a Broadway show in 1921, was made into a silent movie in 1923, and remade as a "talkie" with Spencer Tracy in the lead role as a car salesman. What was the movie?
Six-Cylinder Love.

You can't see too much of the '49 Mercury, but who are these moody teenagers and what was the movie?
James Dean, and Natalie Wood in Rebel Without a Cause.

Chitty-Chitty-Bang-Bang was written by an author more famous for his spy-thrillers. Was it John Buchan, John Le Carré, or Ian Fleming?
Ian Fleming.

Chitty-Chitty-Bang-Bang was based on a real car with that name. The real car raced successfully at Brooklands in the early twenties. Who built and raced it?
Count Louis Zborowski. The car was built on a massive Mercedes chassis and was powered by a 23-litre Maybach Zeppelin engine.

Before Batman got it, was the Batmobile: a Lincoln Futura, a Cadillac Coupe de Ville, or a Chrysler Imperial?
A 1955 Lincoln Futura.

The same vehicle had appeared on screen before. What was the occasion?

It was featured in the 1959 movie It Started with a Kiss, *with Debbie Reynolds.*

Who wrote the book, *On A Clear Day, You Can See General Motors*?
John Z. DeLorean

What make of car sponsored Groucho Marx's radio and TV shows, "You Bet Your Life": Pontiac, De Soto, or Ford?
De Soto.

What group had a hit with "Little Deuce Coupe" in 1963?
The Beach Boys.

What vehicle does TV's "MacGyver" drive?
A Jeep Wrangler.

What car did Ben Braddock (Dustin Hoffman) drive in the movie *The Graduate*?
An Alfa Romeo.

Fred MacMurray makes a hard landing.

THE CAR IN ENTERTAINMENT

In the 1968 movie *Bullitt*, what car did Steve McQueen drive in the famous chase scene?
A Mustang 390 GT.

What car were the "bad guys" driving in the same sequence?
A 440 Magnum Dodge Charger.

Broderick Crawford and Judy Holliday starred in this 1958 film classic, *The Solid Gold...*
Cadillac.

Fred McMurray "flew" this Flivver in *The Absent-Minded Professor*. What was it?
A 1915 Model T Ford.

What car did "Magnum PI" keep borrowing?
A Ferrari.

What car did James Bond (Sean Connery) use in the movie *Goldfinger*?
An Aston Martin DB5.

What car did James Bond use in the book *Goldfinger*?
An Aston Martin DB MK III. Very few of these cars — based on the DB3 RS sports racing car — were made, and there were none available for the 1964 movie. DB5s were therefore used instead.

Another "James Bond" — Roger Moore — appeared in a British TV series as "The Saint". What car did he use?
A Volvo P-1800.

What car did Peter Falk use in his TV role as "Columbo"?
A Peugeot 403 Cabriolet in about the same condition as his raincoat.

007's famous "wheels" in *Goldfinger*.

What is the car Archie and Edith sing about in "All in the Family"?
"Gee our old La Salle ran great. Those were the days..."

In the 1953 classic *Mr. Hulot's Holiday*, what was the vehicle Jacques Tati took on his vacation: a 1928 Delage, a 1924 Amilcar, or a 1927 Hotchkiss?
A 1924 Amilcar.

This 1969 Steve McQueen movie featured a 1905 Winton Flyer. What was the movie?
The Reivers.

What vehicle was featured in the 1960s TV series, "The Rat Patrol"? Clue: think of the desert.
A wartime Jeep.

In this 1955 Chuck Berry hit, a Ford V-8 "bests" a Cadillac Coupe de Ville. What is the name of the song?
"Maybelline".

In the 1955 movie *To Catch a Thief*, Grace Kelly took Cary Grant for a ride along the Grand Corniche in an open sports car. What was it?
A Sunbeam Talbot.

In this 1955 movie, what vehicle did Spencer Tracy drive to his "showdown" in *Bad Day at Black Rock*?
A Jeep.

What car did Kookie (Ed Byrnes) drive in the TV series "77 Sunset Strip"?
A customized Model T Ford.

James Bond has trashed a lot of cars in his movie exploits. What was the vehicle in *For Your Eyes Only* that

The favourite mount of British TV's "The Saint".

developed submarine qualities?
A Lotus Esprit.

In the first James Bond movie, *Dr. No*, Sean Connery is given a few bumps in the back before sending the bad guys over a cliff. What was he driving?
A Sunbeam Alpine.

Martin Milner and George Maharis met with a lot of adventure while driving on "Route 66". What car did they drive in this TV series: a Ford Thunderbird, a Chevrolet Corvette, or a Plymouth Barracuda?
Chevrolet Corvette.

Guests got around "Fantasy Island" in this doorless station wagon. What was it: a Mercury Montego, a Chevrolet Belair, or a Plymouth Volare?
A 1978 Plymouth Volare.

What was the cause of the "creeps" in the movie Christine?
A 1958 Plymouth Fury.

In the movie *Grand Theft Auto*, Ron Howard entered this classic in a demolition derby. What was it?
A Rolls-Royce.

There were lots of cars in *It's A Mad, Mad, Mad, Mad World*. See how many you can identify:
- What was the car that went over the cliff with Jimmy Durante?
- What vehicle did Jonathan Winters drive?
- Mickey Rooney's car was the right size.
- Milton Berle went "topless".
- Sid Caesar had a wagonful.

From the top: a 1957 Ford, a Ford truck, a VW Beetle, a 1962 Imperial convertible, a 1962 Plymouth wagon.

That's Herman (Fred Gwynne) behind the wheel, with Lily (Yvonne de Carlo) beside him. In the back seat are Marylin (Beverly Owen) and Eddie (Butch Patrick). Grandpa (Al Lewis) is hidden by the roof support. So what is the vehicle?
The Munster Koach.

AUTOMANIA

In the 1974 movie *Man With the Golden Gun*, James Bond starts a chase by driving this new car through the showroom window. What was the car?
A Hornet Hatchback.

In the movie of the same name, the "Blues Brothers" seriously re-modeled a shopping mall in this car. What was it?
A 1974 Dodge Monaco.

Peter Fonda "totalled" this car by driving into a train at the conclusion of the movie *Dirty Mary, Crazy Larry*. What was the vehicle?
A 1969 Dodge Charger.

This same scene was shown over and over again in the opening credits of what TV series?
"The Fall Guy".

What car went over the cliff in *The China Syndrome*?

A 1973 Chevrolet Vega.

What was the car used by "The Dukes of Hazzard" in the TV series of the same name?
A 1969 Dodge Charger.

What nickname did they give the car?
General Lee.

What was the number on the side of the car?
"01".

What car did the Beaver's Dad drive in the opening series of "Leave It To Beaver"?
A 1957 Ford.

The movie *American Graffiti* provided many supporting roles for automobiles. How many can you identify?
– What was the car Ron Howard loaned to "Toad"?
– Harrison Ford cruised around in this customized special.

"Put your back into it!" Kenneth More gives typical encouragement to Kay Kendal in *Genevieve*.

THE CAR IN ENTERTAINMENT

– Suzanne Sommers taunted Richard Dreyfuss in this car.

– This car got doused in shaving creme.

– This car was owned by Cindy Williams' parents.

From the top: 1958 Chevrolet Impala; 1955 customized Chevrolet; 1957 Thunderbird; 1960 Cadillac; 1958 Edsel Corsair.

In the opening shots of the TV series "Hill Street Blues", what car comes out of the police garage?
A 1975 Dodge Royal Monaco.

What car did TV's "Baretta" drive: a 1966 Chevrolet, a 1965 Dodge Charger, or a 1964 Ford Torino?
A 1966 Chevrolet.

What was the car in the TV series "Car 54, Where Are You?" Was it a 1959 AMC Ambassador, a 1960 Plymouth, or a 1961 Ford Crown Victoria?
A 1960 Plymouth.

What was the name of the Green Hornet's car?
"The Black Beauty".

What was it before: a 1962 Lincoln Futura, a 1964 Chrysler Imperial, or a 1960 Cadillac Special?
A 1964 Chrysler Imperial.

In the original TV series "Get Smart", agent Maxwell Smart drove this car. Was it a Lotus Elite, a Triumph TR-4, or a Sunbeam Tiger?
A Sunbeam Tiger.

Following a change in the program's principal sponsor, the Sunbeam Tiger was replaced by what car?
A VW Karmann-Ghia.

What was the name of the TV "cops and robbers" show in which the heroes drove a Rolls-Royce?
"Burke's Law"

A close call for "The Jackal". This is before he painted the car.

AUTOMANIA

TV's popular "Knight-Rider" series made an overnight star of this vehicle. What was it?
A Firebird Trans-Am, modified.

The car was run by a "thinking" computer. What was its name?
K.I.T.T.

What did the initials stand for?
Knight Industry Two Thousand.

The Beach Boys had another hit in 1964. "Fun, Fun, Fun" featured the adventures of a girl and her...
Ford T-Bird.

"Speedo" and "Zoom" were popular on the charts in '55 and '56, as performed by this car-named group. Who were they?
The Cadillacs.

The 1953 British movie *Genevieve* is centred around an annual automotive event in England. What is the event?
The London to Brighton Run.

The part of "Genevieve" was played by this veteran auto. Was it a 1906 Spyker, a 1905 Darracq, or a 1904 Simplex?
A 1905 Darracq. Driven by Kenneth More, during the event it is involved in a highly illegal race with John Gregson's 1906 Spyker.

Leaping tall buildings at a single bound was only one of the stunts pulled off by these vehicles in Michael Caine's *The Italian Job*. They were painted red, white and blue. What were they?
Three Austin Minis.

In the very puzzling British TV series "The Prisoner", starring Patrick McGoohan, the opening scene showed a small sports car being driven at high speed across a deserted airfield. What was the car?
A Lotus Seven.

Based on an Upton Sinclair novel, *The Gnome-Mobile* told the story of two homeless gnomes seeking their lost colony in the California Redwoods. What car did they use? Was it a 1930 Rolls-Royce, a 1932 Packard, or a 1934 Stutz?
A 1930 Rolls-Royce.

"Herbie" was a car that had a mind of its own and frequently ignored its drivers. What was "Herbie"?
A VW Beetle.

"Herbie" had a long life in the series of Disney adventures including *The Love Bug, Herbie,* and *Herbie Rides Again.* What was the fourth movie in the series?
Herbie Goes to Monte Carlo.

In the movie *The Three Hundred Yard Drive*, W.C. Fields attempts to play a round of golf while driving this vehicle. Was it a Model T Ford, a Reo, or an American Bantam?
An American Bantam.

In the 1966 movie *Grand Prix* that closely followed the actual 1965 Grand Prix season, James Garner, Yves Montand and Brian Bedford were "mirrored" by actual drivers on the circuit. Who were they imitating?
Garner: Chris Amon; Montand: John Surtees; Bedford: Jackie Stewart.

THE CAR IN ENTERTAINMENT

In this movie, who finally won the World Driver's Championship?
Pete Aron (James Garner) for Yamura.

In the movie *Psycho*, Janet Leigh leaves town in a 1956 Ford but then trades it in on another car. What is the other car?
A 1957 Ford.

Charlie Chaplin fails to get the girl in spite of having this car for *The Jitney Elopement*. What was it?
A Model T Ford.

In the 1971 movie *Vanishing Point*, Barry Newman ends his cross-country chase by crashing into a roadblock. What car was he driving?
A Dodge Challenger.

What did the roadblock consist of?
Two earth-movers.

A hit song in 1905, it helped this company's sales immensely. Bing Crosby revived it in the 1939 movie biography of its composer, Gus Edwards. What was the song?
"In My Merry Oldsmobile".

In the most recent Bond movie, *License To Kill*, 007 has a new set of wheels. Is he driving a Lamborghini Countach, a Mercedes-Benz 560 SEC, or a Continental Mk.VII SC?
A Continental Mk.VII SC.

What car does Sherman Hemsley step out of at the beginning of every TV show in the series "Amen"?
An Oldsmobile 98.

In the movie *Broadcast News*, William Hurt tells his date, "Tonight you're with the best driver and the best car in all of Washington." What is the car?
An Oldsmobile.

The tour of Universal Studios had a special display to publicize their TV series, "The Six Million Dollar Man". It featured a life-like model of Lee Majors lifting a vehicle off the ground. What was the vehicle?
A GMC truck.

In Steve Thompson's book *Recovery*, hero Max Moss slips into Eastern Europe to rescue a "downed" pilot. What vehicle does he use?
A Jeep.

"The Jackal", in the book *Day of the Jackal*, repaints this car by hand to avoid discovery. What is the car?
An Alfa Romeo.

What colour does he paint it?
Blue (it was white).

No company wanted to provide a car for the Steve Martin–John Candy movie *Planes, Trains and Automobiles*, because the vehicle is ridiculed. So the film company just went out and bought a car. What was the lucky company?
Chrysler. They bought six Dodge sedans for the movie.

What was the final fate of the car?
After suffering many indignities, including burning, it is abandoned beside the highway.

Bond Again. In *You Only Live Twice*, 007 is taken for a brisk ride by an Eastern colleague in this radar-equipped roadster. What was it: a Mazda RX-7, a Nissan 240-Z, or a Toyota GT 2000?
A Toyota GT 2000.

CHAPTER 4 VETERAN, VINTAGE & CLASSIC

While many of the early automotive pioneers made enormous contributions to the development of the automobile, only a handful were to survive the first fifty years. In many cases, the inventor/manufacturer simply did not have the capital required to become a viable business and he had to either sell his idea to someone else, merge with another company, or simply drop out. The early cars were expensive propositions that only the very rich could afford, and even they were subject to economic pressures. World War I and the Depression that followed in the early twenties didn't help either.

Veteran automobiles are those that emerged from the very beginning, up to and including the First World War. Vintage vehicles came on the scene between 1919 and the mid-thirties. "Classics" are a judgment call; the Classic Car Club of America considers only certain makes and models between 1925 and 1948 but not everyone agrees with that time frame.

Cars were built in many different places. For example, where were these veteran autos manufactured?
Hotchkiss
Metalurgique
Pungs-Finch
Sunbeam-Mabley
From the top: France, 1912, Belgium, 1900; U.S.A., 1904, and England, 1901.

Many of the great "classic" cars which have enriched the history of the automobile and become, in a sense, "part of the language", had very short

The total lack of protection in this 1907 Pungs-Finch may explain the marque's early demise.

lives. Bentley is a good example. Founded by W.O. Bentley, the first car appeared in 1919. How many years did Bentley flourish: 11, 13, or 16?

Only eleven years. In spite of the marque's great prestige, its numerous records and five outright wins at Le Mans, it foundered in the late twenties and was taken over by another company.

During its brief life, Bentley produced a total of how many cars: 3,061, 5,859, or 11,205?

Only 3,061.

What was the company that took over Bentley in 1931?

Rolls-Royce.

One of the most famous Bentley models was the 1930 4-1/2 litre model fitted with a supercharger. At whose instigation was the supercharger fitted?

Race driver Sir Henry Birkin, who drove one of them to second place in the French GP that year.

What was surprising about the installation of the Amherst-Villiers superchargers in this model?

Although the factory built fifty with this modification, W.O. Bentley did not approve. According to W.O., "...to supercharge a Bentley engine was to pervert its design and corrupt its performance...."

Perhaps the most famous of all hood ornaments is to be found on the Rolls-Royce. What is its correct name?

"The Spirit of Ecstasy".

A 4-1/2 litre Bentley with an Amherst-Villiers supercharger mounted behind the license plate.

AUTOMANIA

The design was commissioned in 1911. Why did Rolls-Royce want a hood ornament after six years without one?
Owners were putting their own hood ornaments on the cars, and most were not considered "suitable" by the R-R Board of Directors.

Who was the artist they commissioned?
Sculptor Charles Sykes.

Who was the model?
Eleanor Thornton, private secretary to Lord Montagu of Beaulieu who was on the R-R Board of Directors. However, this is contested by Sykes' daughter.

How many different designs of the "Spirit of Ecstasy" have been used on Rolls-Royce cars: one, two, or four?
Four. The first had a more upright stance and was used on the 40/50 models between 1911–1926. The second, and most common, was introduced in 1922 for the smaller 20/25 models. In 1935 a version known as "The Kneeling Lady" — for obvious reasons — was featured on the Phantom III series. The most recent version was introduced in 1955.

The most famous hood ornament of all time. But don't call her "The Flying Lady". Those are not wings, but the folds of her diaphanous gown billowing behind her. The superb detail is achieved by the "lost wax" process, a technique that goes back to Babylonian days.

VETERAN, VINTAGE & CLASSIC

The great reputation of Rolls-Royce was built on the "Silver Ghost" model. When was it introduced: 1904, 1906, or 1909?
1906.

How long did it remain in production: 12 years, 16 years, or 20 years?
20 years, with minor modifications.

What car company used as its emblem a serpent swallowing a Saracen?
Alfa Romeo.

What was the significance of this symbol?
The Crusaders from Milan went into battle against the Saracens with a banner showing this device. Subsequently it was incorporated into the city of Milan's "arms" that is the basis of the Alfa emblem.

What company uses Neptune's Trident as its emblem?
Maserati.

What company used a griffin as its emblem: Delage, Vauxhall, or Humber?
Vauxhall.

From the arms of the house of Baracca.

The A.L.F.A. company was incorporated in 1909. What do the letters stand for?
Anonima Lombardo Fabbrica Automobili.

Nicola Romeo reorganized the company as Alfa Romeo in 1919, 1923, or 1926?
1919.

Fulke's Hall is the origin of what British make?
It became Vauxhall, where car production began in 1903.

Everyone is familiar with the black, prancing horse symbol of Ferrari. Where does the symbol come from?
It is part of the coat of arms of the Baracca family. Francesco Baracca was a fighter ace, killed in WWI. Following an impressive win by Ferrari at the 1923 Circuit of Salvio, in Ravenna, he was presented with the crest by Francesco's parents. It then became the official symbol of Scuderia Ferrari.

What is Ferrari's first name?
Enzo.

What were the cars first raced by the Scuderia Ferrari?
Alfa Romeos.

The first model bearing the Ferrari name appeared in 1931, 1939, or 1947?
The first true Ferrari (the Tipo 125) appeared in 1947, with its characteristic V-12 engine designed by Gioachino Colombo. Early models in the thirties such as the Ferrari ''Bimotore'', were simply modified Alfas.

What car company used a rampant elephant for a hood ornament: Hispano-Suiza, Bugatti, or Lagonda?
Bugatti, but only on the Royales.

How many Bugatti Royales were produced: one, six, or seventeen?
Six.

The Bugatti Royales were built specifically for the crowned heads of

One of the only six ever produced, this Bugatti was meant for ''royal personages''.

Europe. How many "royals" purchased these cars?
None.

Which of these American classics came first: the Corvette or the Thunderbird?
The Chevrolet Corvette appeared in 1953 and the Ford Thunderbird two years later.

What vintage American company used a bounding jack-rabbit as its emblem? Was it Duryea, Apperson, or Winton?
Apperson.

What classic cars come out of the factory at Newport Pagnell?
Aston Martin.

A raging bull was chosen to symbolize the vehicles of this Italian manufacturer. Who is it?
Lamborghini.

What does Citröen's "Double Chevron" radiator badge signify?
It represents the interlocking teeth of bevelled gears, commemorating Andre Citröen's previous trade.

This company chose the head of the Egyptian sun-god Ra as its hood emblem. Was it Locomobile, Marmon, or Stutz?
Stutz.

This archer was the hood emblem of what classic American automobile?
Pierce-Arrow.

AUTOMANIA

The flying stork hood emblem belongs to Hispano-Suiza, Isotta-Franschini, or Packard?
Hispano-Suiza.

Where did the symbol come from?
La Cigogne Volante, the symbol of Lorraine, was used as the squadron emblem of the famous WWI fighter escadrille commanded by French ace Georges Guynemer. They flew Spad fighters equipped with Hispano-Suiza engines and because of this connection, the symbol was adopted by the car company.

Daimler was taken over by what British company in 1960?
Jaguar.

What company chose the head of Egypt's Sphinx for its hood emblem: Delahaye, Leyland, or Armstrong-Siddeley?
Armstrong-Siddeley.

Who was responsible for the Ford Thunderbird design: Virgil Exner, Raymond Leowy, or Frank Hershey?
Frank Hershey.

The Mohs Seaplane Company of Madison, Wisconsin, built several very expensive — and bizarre — limousines between 1968 and 1977. They featured 5-litre and 9-litre engines, rear door entry and every conceivable luxury. What was the sedan called?
Mohs Ostentatienne Opera Sedan.

Before establishing its own dealer body, what American car company was named the exclusive distributor for Mercedes-Benz in 1958?
Studebaker-Packard.

One other company used the Flying Stork symbol of Hispano-Suiza. What was the company? Clue: it involved

another WWI fighter ace.
Fonck. Named for Rene Fonck, the top Allied fighter ace of WWI who also flew in the Cigogne Volante Escadrille. Despite his enormous popularity, the car was not a success, only 12 being made between 1920 and 1925.

When did the first Porsche appear: 1939, 1949, or 1951?
The Porsche 356 was introduced at the 1949 Geneva Auto Salon.

Who was responsible for the design of the Porsche 356: Ferdinand or his son, Ferry?
Ferry Porsche, although the genesis of the marque can be traced to the "Berlin-Rome" streamlined, VW-based coupe that was built by Dr. Ferdinand Porsche in 1938-39.

Why was the Jaguar XK 120 so-called when it was introduced in 1948?

Because William Lyons of Jaguar guaranteed it would reach 120 mph in stock form.

Did it live up to this expectation?
It did better, reaching a speed of 132.6 mph in the spring of 1949, on a stretch of European highway.

Where did the record take place?
Jabbeke in Belgium.

Who drove the Jaguar on its record run?
Jaguar tester Ron "Soapy" Sutton.

Who was known as "Il Commendatore"?
Enzo Ferrari.

When did Fiat finally take over Ferrari: 1969, 1974, or 1976?
Fiat acquired controlling interest in 1969.

1921 Apperson with "cheesecake" of the period.

AUTOMANIA

The mid-engined, V-6 Ferrari Dino was introduced in 1967. What is the significance of the name "Dino"?
The name is in memory of Ferrari's son, Dino, who died of leukemia at age 24 in 1954.

The Ferrari Dino was significant in one other respect. Who built the V-6 engines?
Fiat. Fiat began to play an increasingly important role in Ferrari activities through the late sixties and early seventies.

What made the Dino 206 unlike all other Ferraris?
It carried no Ferrari nameplate or prancing horse emblem.

Ettore Bugatti referred to them derisively as "...the fastest trucks in the world." To what was he referring?
Bentley cars. The comment followed Bentley's win in the 1928 24-Hours at Le Mans.

What classic British cars were once built under licence in Springfield, Massachusetts: Daimler, Lagonda, or Rolls-Royce?
Rolls-Royce. Silver Ghosts were built between 1920–26, and Phantoms from 1927 until 1931, when the operation ceased.

Complete these classic names:
_____ Interceptor
_____ Hollywood
_____ Magnette
From the top: Jensen, Graham, MG.

What is the significance of the "810" in the 1936 Cord 810?
It was introduced on the 10th of August (the eighth month).

The Cord L-29 of 1929 utilized front-wheel drive technology from what race car manufacturer?
Miller.

What does Henry Miller's middle initial

You'd be smiling too if you had just taken delivery of this 1936 Cord Sportsman. Who is the lucky lady?
Clue: she was even more at ease on ice.
Skating and movie star Sonja Henie.

"A" stand for?
Armenius.

What was the last model year for De Soto: 1957, 1959, or 1961?
1961.

Fins didn't just appear on fenders. One vehicle even had them on its rear doors. What vehicle was it: a 1957 Lincoln, a 1961 Cadillac, or a 1963 Chrysler Imperial?
A 1957 Lincoln. Mercifully, they were removed in 1958.

What company used a ship's helm as the emblem for its "Clipper" series?
Packard.

Why was the Bentley "Mulsanne" so-called?
After the Mulsanne Straight at Le Mans, scene of Bentley's five wins in the twenties and thirties.

What does the name Hispano-Suiza signify?
It refers to the partnership of Spanish and Swiss enterprise. Marc Birkigt, a talented Swiss engineer, received backing from a group of Barcelona businessmen in 1904, to form Hispano-Suiza.

In 1951, Hispano-Suiza was taken over by another Spanish automotive concern. What was its name?
ENASA — Empresa Nacional de Autocamiones SA.

This company is better known by the expensive and exclusive cars they made between 1951 and 1958. Were they Facel-Vegas, Pegasos, or Ansaldos?
Pegasos.

The British company AC built their first car in 1913. The following year they introduced a remarkable 2.0 litre, 6-cylinder engine that remained in production for a record 36, 44, or 49 years?
49 years. During that time the power was increased from 40 b.h.p. to 103 b.h.p.!

A Springfield Phantom I Rolls-Royce.

AUTOMANIA

What do the initials AC stand for?
Auto Carriers.

Over the years, AC earned an enviable reputation for building stylish, high performance cars; but in 1961, American Carroll Shelby put a small-block V-8 engine into an AC Ace and created one of the most potent sports cars ever. What was it?
The Shelby Cobra.

BMW, long famous for its aero engines, got started in car manufacturing when it took over the Dixi company in 1928. Dixi was the name given to a popular British make which BMW continued to make under license. What was the British car?
The Austin Seven.

What was the special relationship between Bentley and Aston Martin? Clue: it surfaced after David Brown bought Aston Martin and Lagonda.
When W.O. Bentley left the company bearing his name, he went to work for Lagonda and built them a superb DOHC, 2.6 litre engine. Promptly installed in the new DB Aston

Rare and expensive, the Pegaso Berline of 1958.

This British sports car from AC of Thames Ditton, was to get a second life from Carroll Shelby.

Martin, it became the basis of their future racing successes.

Many fine cars of the thirties — particularly French — featured superbly crafted hood ornaments in glass. What was the name of the glass maker?
Lalique.

In the early 1900s, Smith & Mabley of New York were importers of Mercedes and Panhard. But the 40 percent import tax made these vehicles prohibitively expensive, even for the well-heeled "sports" in those income-tax free days. They decided that they could build a comparable car for much less. What was the car they built: Locomobile, Simplex, or Mercer?
Simplex.

What was the car they used as a model?
The Mercedes.

"If you're so smart, why don't you build a car yourself!" It was this remark, made to James Ward Packard, that led to the birth of this famous marque in 1899. Who made the comment? Was it Henry Ford, Alexander Winton, or Ransom Olds?
It was Alexander Winton. Packard had bought a Winton "Horseless" which drove him crazy by continually breaking down. The remark was made after Packard expressed his low opinion of Winton workmanship.

Rubbing it in. Less than a month after a Winton had set the record, a Packard — "Old Pacific" — beat it by three days. What was the event?
The first trans-continental crossing of America by automobile. The Winton did it

first, in 64 days. Tom Fetch in "Old Pacific" did it in 61 days.

These luxury cars were shipped in dust-proof paper bags, installed in covered freight cars which had been scrupulously swept clean beforehand. Were they Rolls-Royce, Cadillac, or Lincoln cars?
Lincolns. These standards were introduced by Edsel Ford, following the acquisition of Lincoln in 1921.

Can you complete these classic names?
_____ Red Label
_____ Silver Dawn
_____ SSKL
From the top: Bentley, Rolls-Royce, Mercedes.

The "London-Edinburgh" model of this marque was so-called after running from London to Edinburgh in 1911 in top gear only! What was the make?
Rolls-Royce.

The Bulldog, Bearcat and Black Hawk were all models made by this American company. Name the company.
Stutz.

Identify these classics:
_____ Lamba
_____ Super America
_____ Type 35B
From the top: Lancia, Ferrari, Bugatti.

And what about these?
_____ Le Mans Replica
Prince Henry _____
_____ Raceabout
From the top: Frazer-Nash, Vauxhall, Mercer.

What was the company that took over Packard in 1954? Clue: it was located in South Bend.
Studebaker and Packard merged to form Studebaker-Packard Corporation.

When did the Packard name finally disappear from the scene: 1958, 1960, or 1965?
1958.

What do these model names have in common: Citation, Pacer, Ranger and Corsair?
They were all model names used on the Edsel series.

What car of 1928–31 featured the profiles of the three founders on its its hood badge?
Graham-Paige.

What were the names of the three Graham brothers?
Ray A., Robert C., and Joseph C.

What's it worth? The 1989 Christie's auction in Monte Carlo set some new values for some old classics. Match these prices to the cars:
'57 Aston Martin
DBR 2 sports racing car $1.7M
'34 3.2-litre, Alfa Romeo $0.864M
Tipo B, monoposto $3.2M
'56 3.4-litre, Jaguar $3.6M
D-Type
'66 4.7-litre, Ford GT 40
From the top: $3.6M, $3.2M, $1.7M, $0.864M

"The Goddess of Speed" emblem graced the hood of these cars from 1926 to 1950 the longest continuous use of such an ornament. Did it belong to Studebaker, Buick or Packard?
Irreverently known as "The Doughnut Pusher", it belonged to Packard.

Abingdon was the home of what British sports car Morgan, MG or Triumph?
MG

CHAPTER 5 ✣ THE CAR IN CULTURE

The automobile has become a pervasive force in our daily lives. As the car became commonplace, it brought with it many other trappings — not all beneficial — such as thruways, "road-food", stoplights, breathalyser tests, drive-in movies, radar traps and gridlock. And, of course, the parking meter.

When was the first parking meter unveiled: 1932, 1935, or 1938?
1935.

Where was it installed: New York City, Los Angeles, or Oklahoma City?
Oklahoma City.

Standard Oil of Ohio opened the first filling station in Cincinnati in 1910, 1912, or 1915?
1912.

How did motorists "gas up" before this?
Before the advent of "filling stations", motorists had to purchase fuel from coal merchants, lumber yards, hardware stores and pharmacies.

When did the first drive-in movie theatre open for business: 1929, 1933, or 1936?
1933.

Where was it located: Camden, NJ, Rochester, NY, or Hollywood, CA?
Camden, NJ.

The first cab fleet in the world was plying for hire as early as 1897. Where would you have hailed one of these cabs: London, Paris, or New York?
London. The London Electric Cab Company, with 77 cabs designed by Walter Bersey, was in business for three years before competition forced them to close.

The long arm of the law. George "Red" Compton of Williamsport, Pennsylvania, found his cruiser "a restful change" from his Harley-Davidson. What is it?
A 1928 Studebaker.

AUTOMANIA

What was the competition?
Horses. The electric cabs were too slow to compete with London's hansom cabs.

The first "royal" motorist went for a spin in 1893. Who was it: England's Prince of Wales, King Alfonso XIII of Spain, or Kaiser Wilhelm of Germany?
England's Prince of Wales was taken for a ride by the French chocolate manufacturer Gaston Menier in his steam Serpollet.

Who said of her first encounter with an automobile, "A very shaky and disagreeable conveyance altogether". Clue: she was not amused.
Queen Victoria. Which is probably why the Prince of Wales had to wait six years and become Edward VII before he could buy one!

When did the first drive-in church open for services: 1938, 1945, or 1958?
1958.

Where was it located? Of course it was in California, but where?
Garden Grove, CA.

Who opened the first "turnpike" restaurant: Wendy's, Stuckey's, or Howard Johnson?
Howard Johnson.

Where was it located?
On the Pennsylvania Turnpike.

When did it open: 1936, 1938, or 1940?
1940.

What country is signified by the international registration plate CH?
Switzerland (Confederatio Helvetia).

Where do (did) these cars come from:

Pegaso, Skoda and Sabra?
Spain, Czechoslovakia, and Israel.

What 1929 automobile was named after a U.S. president?
The Marmon Roosevelt.

What countries were responsible for these makes?
Bucciali
Clyno
Adler
Tatra
From the top: France, England, Germany, and Czechoslovakia.

In what year did the U.S. introduce the "Double Nickel" and what is it?
The 55 mph speed limit was introduced in August 1977.

What department of the government was responsible for it?
The National Highway Traffic Safety Administration.

British Daimlers were made the "royal" cars by Edward VII in 1900. They remained so until this monarch made a change. Was it George V, George VI, or Elizabeth II?
Elizabeth II in 1968.

What was the car she chose to replace Daimler: Humber, Rolls-Royce, or Jaguar?
Rolls-Royce.

Asphalt was first used on the roads of Babylon 600 years before Christ. It was "re-discovered" by American A.L. Barber in 1877, 1880, or 1885?
1877.

Barber secured the rights to a huge

deposit of pitch on a Caribbean island. What was the island?
Trinidad.

By 1896 his company had laid almost half of all the pavement in the U.S., and Barber became known as "The Asphalt King". What do his initials "A.L." stand for?
Amzi Lorenzo.

Barber used his wealth to launch one of America's most prestigious car makes in 1899. Was it Chadwick, Locomobile, or Peerless?
Locomobile.

In 1957 this company featured the first "disappearing" hardtop called the "Skyliner". Was it Chrysler, Oldsmobile, or Ford?
Ford.

What car was President John F. Kennedy riding in when he was assassinated: a Lincoln, a Cadillac, or a Custom Imperial?
A 1961 Lincoln Continental, customized by Hess & Eisenhardt.

What country is signified by the international license plate AUS?
Australia.

It's a 1927 Packard Phaeton, about to start a parade up Broadway, New York City. Who is the celebrity in the back?
Charles Lindbergh. The parade was to honor his solo flight across the Atlantic.

AUTOMANIA

When oil-millionairess Sandra West died in 1977, she left her fortune to her brother-in-law Sol West, on condition she be buried "in my lace night-gown and in my (car), with the seat slanted comfortably..." What was the car?
Her Ferrari. Sol West complied and also covered the car in nine feet of concrete.

Companies come, go and are sometimes taken over. Who now owns Citröen, Jeep, and Ferrari?
Peugeot, Chrysler, and Fiat.

The shot "heard around the world", was fired by Gavrilio Princip, at Sarajevo in 1914, when he assassinated Archduke Ferdinand and Duchess Sophie. What car were they riding in at the time: a Mercedes, a Graf & Stift, or a Steyr-Puch?
An Austrian Graf & Stift.

Motels brought overnight accommodation to the traveller by locating on the highway. When did the first Holiday Inn open? Was it 1948, 1950, or 1952?
1952.

Where was it located?
Memphis, Tennessee.

Driving tests were first inaugurated in this country. Was it France, Britain, or Denmark?
France.

What U.S. states use(d) these license plate slogans?
Land of Lincoln
The Show Me State
The Great Lakes State
From the top: Illinois, Missouri, Michigan.

Gertrude Hope and Miriam Leland Woodbridge enjoying a spin in a "toy" Cadillac, the marque created by their grandfather, Henry Leland. This model was originally owned by Prince Olaf of Norway and was given to Wilfred Leland, Jr, on his fifth birthday, on April 6, 1913 — about the time this photograph was taken.

What famous makes are manufactured here?
Linkoping
Maranello
Toledo
From the top: Saab, Ferrari, Jeep.

What twenties bank robber wrote a testimonial letter to Henry Ford, complimenting him on making such great "getaway cars"?
Clyde Barrow, of Bonnie and Clyde. John Dillinger also spoke highly of Ford cars.

What car was destroyed by the book Unsafe At Any Speed?
Although subsequently exonerated by the U.S. Department of Transport, Chevrolet's Corvair was pretty well forced off the road by this book.

Who wrote the book?
Ralph Nader.

Where was the first sequential traffic light installed: Detroit, London, or New York?
Detroit.

What year was it installed: 1912, 1919, or 1923?
1919.

Englishman Loraine Barrow died as a result of injuries sustained in the disastrous Paris-Madrid race of 1903. When his heirs tried to collect on his insurance they were refused and had to sue the insurance company. Why?
Because he had not disclosed that he was a "racing motorist". For "occupation", he had simply entered "Gentleman" on the application form. The judge ruled that racing was a normal occupation for a gentleman and the insurance company had to pay up.

The car that Ralph Nader "wouldn't buy".

AUTOMANIA

What Detroit car company introduced the "La Femme" model in 1955, complete with comb, purse, compact and lipstick — all in pink, of course?
Chrysler. It was based on the Newport model and survived only two years.

When General Motors introduced the Nova in 1969, it heralded the launch of a new generation of "compact" cars. What was significant about the Nova name?
Each individual letter of the word "Nova" was the initial of the new family of "compacts".

Can you identify each of those names?
Chevrolet Nova, Oldsmobile Omega, Pontiac Ventura, and Buick Apollo.

What was the penalty for speeding in Peking in 1938: life suspension of license, one year hard labor, or death?
Death.

The perpetrators of the St. Valentine's Day Massacre in 1929 drove to the scene of the crime in a vehicle disguised to look like something else. Was it a Chevrolet, a Ford or a Packard? And what did it appear to be?
A Packard Tourer, disguised as a police car.

Although left-hand steering became commonplace in Europe and the U.S.A., many of the very expensive makes continued to put the steering wheel on the right, as late as the 1950s. Why?
Because it was more convenient for chauffeurs who had to open and close the passenger side door for their employers. Bugatti never built a left-hand drive car; Lancia only changed over to left-hand steering in 1956.

What was the unique visual feature of the 1930 Willys-Knight "Plaidside" roadster?
The side body panels were finished in a tartan fabric. But it wasn't the first time. The French firm of Voisin did the same thing in 1920.

Where was the first modern motorway built: the United States, Germany, or Italy?
No, not Germany. It was a 21 km stretch of Autostrada between Milan and Varese, Italy.

When was it opened: 1920, 1924, or 1929?
1924.

Germany's first Autobahn stretched from Darmstadt to Frankfurt and was opened in 1930, 1934, or 1937?
1934.

The first "turnpike" in the United States didn't open until 1940. What was it called?
The Pennsylvania Turnpike.

Britain's first modern motorway was the Preston Bypass. Was it opened in 1948, 1950, or 1958?
1958.

"Any man or woman, 18 years of age or over, of good moral character and respectable standing, friendly to the motor vehicle and its interests" could join this association for $2.00 in 1895. What was it?
The American Motor League, the first general membership motor club in the world.

What is "The Flying Squad"?
Scotland Yard's famous mobile police squad, formed in 1920.

THE CAR IN CULTURE

Who was the writer in the forties and fifties who did road test reports for Mechanix Illustrated?
Tom McCahill.

In 1971 this car came with a key that was also a tool kit. It featured a spark plug gapper, Phillips screwdriver, distributor and spark plug gauge, and a one and a half inch ruler. What was the car?
1971 Ford Pinto.

Match these cars to their factory home towns:

Pierce-Arrow	Lansing, MI
Viking	Detroit, MI
Essex	Cincinnati, OH
Crosley	Buffalo, NY

From the top: Buffalo, Lansing, Detroit, and Cincinnati.

The first commercial oil strike in North America took place here in 1858. Was it in Oil Springs, Ontario, Titusville, Pennsylvania, or Spindletop, Texas?
Oil Springs, Ontario.

Buying with time payments began back in the 1850s with Singer Sewing Machines. What company first used time payments for its car purchases?
Studebaker.

In what year: 1903, 1909, or 1911?
1911.

What was the first car company to set up its own credit division to provide this service to customers: General Motors, Studebaker, or Willys?
The John North Willys Security Corp. was set up in 1916. The General Motors Acceptance Corp. began operations three years later.

Only the French would do it. This cross between a bus and a train, named "Micheline" — note the Michelin tire-clad wheels — ran from Paris to Deauville on rails in 2 hr. 3 min., at an average speed of 207 kph. The body is by Carrosserie Wibault and the car is powered by a Hispano-Suiza engine.

What was the "shunpike"?
Any secondary road that avoided the tolls on the "turnpike".

The Boston Symphony Orchestra created a furor in 1927 when it performed this original work by T. Converse. Conductor Serge Koussevitsky protested at the numerous honks, rattles, bangs and explosions in the score, but the composer insisted they were essential to the work. Entitled "Flivver Ten Million", what did the work celebrate?
It was in honour of the ten millionth Model T Ford. Don't look for it on compact disc.

Few European companies have been consistent successes in North America. Renault's major post-WWII attempt failed miserably in 1959 with the death of this sub-compact. Was it the Fregate, the Aronde, or the Dauphine?
The Dauphine met with great success initially but couldn't take the hard North American usage. Renault also failed to prepare a solid dealer body, or provide adequate parts and service.

Renault's second attempt to penetrate the North American market came in 1978 when it purchased shares in what American company?
American Motors.

In spite of the tremendous success of Jeep vehicles, Renault was unable to get a foothold in the passenger car market and sold its shares in American Motors. Was it eight, nine, or ten years later?
Nine years later (1987).

A 1929 Olds Viking, posed in the right demographic surroundings.

✤

What American company bought the AMC shares from Renault?
The Chrysler Corporation.

This was the biggest consolidation in the North American automobile industry since the merger of the Hudson and Nash-Kelvinator companies that created American Motors in 1954. Perhaps that's why Chrysler's other acquisition that year went almost unnoticed. What prestigious Italian automaker did Chrysler buy in 1987?
Lamborghini.

Famed British explorer Sir Ernest Shackleton named this Antarctic glacier in honor of the major sponsor of his unsuccessful attempt to reach the South Pole in 1908. Was it Henry Ford, Sir William Beardmore, or Henry Royce?

The Beardmore Glacier is named after Scottish industrialist Sir William Beardmore, manufacturer of the Beardmore taxi cab.

Elmo L. Geoghan opened the first "drive-in" restaurant in 1936. What was it called?
Bob's Big Boy.

When did the "Golden Arches" first go up: 1934, 1936, or 1937?
Richard and Maurice McDonald opened for business in 1937.

Where was the first McDonald's located?
Pasadena, California.

When Bagwam Shree Rajneesh "took a powder" from his commune in Oregon, he left behind 85 luxury limos. Were they Cadillacs, Mercedes, or Rolls-Royces?
Rolls-Royces.

The Renault Dauphine started out well, outselling VW in 1959, but rust, lack of dealer service and high freeway speeds were its undoing.

What were Pontiacs known as before they were Pontiacs?
Oaklands. General Motors' Billy Durant acquired Oakland in 1908 and the name continued in use until 1931.

What terrorist group took responsibility for the assassination of Renault head George Besse in 1986?
Action Directe. Two men and two women were subsequently sentenced to life imprisonment for this crime.

Who were "The Whiz Kids"?
A group of ten U.S.A.A.F. officers, led by Col. Charles Thornton, from the Office of Statistical Control.

They were experts in modern management systems and they were seeking peacetime employment. **What car company did they approach?**
The Ford Motor Company. They were hired by Henry Ford II and they brought modern management techniques to Ford.

What states or provinces use(d) these license plate messages?
America's Dairyland
Land of the Midnight Sun
Garden of the Gulf
From the top: Wisconsin, The Yukon, and Prince Edward Island.

What country is signified by this international registration plate MO?
Monaco (MC prior to 1962).

In the early fifties, the Kaiser "Henry J" model was sold through the Sears

The perils of winter driving, circa 1910, are evident in this Oakland driver's face as he tries to unstick from a snowdrift.

THE CAR IN CULTURE

Roebuck stores and was listed in their mail order catalogue. What name was it marketed under?
The Allstate.

Where was the Edsel's push-button-operated, automatic transmission located?
In the center of the steering-wheel.

Not too many cars have been "lost at sea" but this 1956 dream car by Ghia went down on the way to its first public showing. Who commissioned this "one-of"? Was it Ford, Nash, or Chrysler?
Chrysler.

What was the name of this dream car?
The Norseman.

Where did it sink?
In the Atlantic Ocean.

What was the ship involved?
The Andrea Doria.

What make/model featured a badge depicting a Roman soldier's helmet?
The Buick Centurion.

What is the name of the Spanish company that built Fiats under license?
SEAT.

Rover began development of its Landrover 4WD vehicles in the late forties. What existing vehicle did it use as a starting point?
The WWII Willys Jeep MB.

Here's how the Sears Roebuck and Co. publicity department captioned this photo. "A distinctive ultra-modern grille with massive air foil louvers marks the style of the new Allstate automobile now being introduced by Sears, Roebuck and Co. Exceptional road visibility is provided by sightseeing safety windshield and the low, sloping hood. Car-width parking lights are located in the fenders."

AUTOMANIA

What states or provinces use(d) these license plate slogans?
The Picture Province
The Heart of Dixie
Land of Enchantment
From the top: New Brunswick, Alabama, and New Mexico.

What countries were home to these makes?
Borgward Isabella
Triangcl
Minerva
Zaporozhetz
From the top: West Germany, Denmark, Belgium, and U.S.S.R.

What is (was) the nationality of these car makes?
Trabant
Holden
Tracta
From the top: West Germany, Australia, and France.

When did Bob White split the Canadian autoworkers away from the UAW and form the CAW: 1984, 1985, or 1986?
September, 1985.

What companies were responsible for these quaint models?
Bi-Autogo
Gold Bug
Lettuce
From the top: Scripps-Booth (U.S.), Kissel (U.S.), and Mitsubishi (Japan).

What vehicles are (were) made in these factories?
Maranello
Ile Seguin
South Bend
From the top: Ferrari, Renault, and Avanti (also Studebaker and Rockne).

Name three companies that have used the "Regal" nameplate.
Buick, Dodge, and Studebaker.

The year is 1929 and General Augusto C. Sandino (in white), the Nicaraguan rebel leader, is seen here on his flight from Nicaragua to Mexico City. What is the car?
A Packard.

THE CAR IN CULTURE

❧

Name three companies that have used the "Alpine" nameplate.
Sunbeam-Talbot, Sunbeam (after the purchase of Sunbeam-Talbot by The Rootes Group), and Renault.

What states or provinces use(d) these license plate slogans?
Famous Potatoes
The Beef State
Je Me Souviens
From the top: Idaho, Nebraska, and Quebec.

The first center-line on a rural highway in North America was painted between Marquette and Ishpeming, Michigan in 1915, 1917, or 1920?
1917.

The Khamsin, Mistral and Ghibli are the names of famous winds. They have also been used to name high performance cars from Lamborghini, Maserati, or Ferrari?
Maserati.

In Britain, members of the Automobile Association were served by motorcycle patrols who would salute cars displaying the AA badge. What did it mean if the patrol did not salute?
It meant that a police speed trap was in operation nearby. This practice died out in the late sixties.

The French company Simca began operating in Nanterre in 1934, with a licensing arrangement to build someone else's car. What was the other car?
Fiat.

"The Funnel of World Commerce" appeared on the license plate of what U.S. Territory?
The Canal Zone.

What was the "Carabella"?
It was a Kaiser made from Kaiser Manhattan body dies in Argentina from 1958 to 1962.

A motorcycle with "training wheels"? A novel approach to economical transportation, the Scripps-Booth Bi-Autogo ought to go, but didn't.

AUTOMANIA

What were Ramblers called in Argentina: Torinos, Cordobas, or Sierras?
Torinos.

What state or province license plates use(d) these slogans?
Yours to Discover
The Corn State
10,000 Lakes
From the top: Ontario, Iowa, and Minnesota.

What country is represented by the international registration plate SF?
Finland.

What countries saw the birth of these marques?
Hyundai
Pic-Pic
Jowett
From the top, South Korea, Switzerland, and Great Britain.

Probably the most bizarre hood ornament in all automotive history was featured on this 1925 British Wolseley. The model was called "The Silent Six". What was the hood ornament?
Six Ku Klux Klansmen standing in a circle. Advertised as a "silent" automobile, owners kept bringing it back for service if they heard anything at all. The company went bankrupt two years later and was taken over by the William Morris Company.

The Austin Seven was the British equivalent of Ford's Model T. Introduced in 1926, this sub-compact economy car was sold under license in several other countries. What names was it marketed under in:

This 1939 model shows that Powell Crosley really meant it when he said he'd build economy cars. Unfortunately, nobody wanted them.

THE CAR IN CULTURE

France
Germany
The United States
Japan
From the top: Rosengart, Dixi, American Bantam, and Datsun.

The first drive-in bank opened in Los Angeles in 1937, 1940 or 1946?
1937.

Why was the Daimler Conquest of 1953 so named?
The Norman Conquest of England took place in 1066. The Daimler Conquest cost exactly £1,066 sterling.

What is the name of the famous road that runs from Lashio, Burma to Kunming, China?
The Burma Road.

What is the name of the famous road that runs from Oberammergau to Wurzburg?
The Romantische Strasse (The Romantic Road).

What is the name of the route that runs between Dawson Creek and Fairbanks?
The Alaska Highway.

What country is signified by the international registration NL?
The Netherlands.

What states use(d) these slogans on their license plates?
The Garden State
The Empire State
Land of Opportunity
From the top: New Jersey, New York, and Arkansas.

France's version of the Austin Seven. A Rosengart Super Five of 1936.

AUTOMANIA

The first Stop sign to control traffic was installed in Detroit in 1914. In the same year, the first electric traffic lights were installed. Was this in Detroit, Cleveland, or New York?
Cleveland, in August 1914.

Women's "lib" got an early boost when Alice Ramsey and three female companions became the first women to drive across the American continent. Their route took them from New York to San Francisco and was completed in 53 days. What was the year: 1909, 1911, or 1915?
1909.

What car did they use? A Chalmers, a Locomobile, or a Maxwell?
A Maxwell.

Who was known as "Le Patron"?
Ettore Bugatti.

What is the origin of the term "chauffeur"?
Early steam-powered vehicles required a "stoker" to tend the boiler. "Stoker", translated into French, the international language of the automobile, is "chauffeur".

In 1865 this country enacted a law that required an automobile to have three drivers, not to exceed 4 mph, and to be preceded by a man on foot carrying a red flag. Was it Britain, Germany or Denmark?
Britain.

Who said, "History is bunk"?
Attributed to Henry Ford, but he refuted it. "I did not say it was bunk...it was bunk to me [referring to his school days], but I didn't need it very much."

Ferdinand Porsche's prototype "People's Car" was on the road as early as 1935.

THE CAR IN CULTURE

❀

It was to be called the Strength Through Joy car; what was it?
The Volkswagen Beetle.

Who designed the Volkswagen: Adolf Hitler, Ferdinand Porsche or Heinz Nordhoff?
Ferdinand Porsche was responsible for the design, although the major impetus for the vehicle came from Adolf Hitler.

Who named the vehicle, the Strength Through Joy car (Kraft durch Freude)?
Adolf Hitler. To the surprise and embarrassment of Ferdinand Porsche, Hitler christened the car when laying the cornerstone at the VW factory in 1938. Kraft durch Freude was the slogan of the National Socialist Labor Front.

Where is the Volkswagen factory located?
Wolfsburg, W. Germany.

Who was the first member of royalty to purchase an automobile: Edward VII of Britain, Kaiser Wilhelm of Germany, or Czar Alexander II of Russia?
In 1864 an agent for Czar Alexander purchased a gas-engined carriage that had been built by Frenchman Etienne Lenoir. It was shipped by rail from Vincennes, France to St. Petersburg.

Who was the first U.S. President to drive to his inauguration: Woodrow Wilson, William H. Taft or Warren G. Harding?
Warren G. Harding.

What was the vehicle he used?
A Packard Twin Six.

Alice Ramsey and her ''all girl'' crew, suitably dressed to take on the continent.

AUTOMANIA

Who was the first President of the United States to formally make the change from horses to automobiles?
William H. Taft.

What vehicles did he acquire for the White House?
A White Steamer, two Pierce-Arrows and a Baker Electric, neatly covering all bets — steam, gasoline and electricity!

Who was the first president of the United States to have a state car bullet-proofed?
Franklin Delano Roosevelt.

What prompted this decision?
A 1933 assassination attempt which cost the life of Chicago Mayor, Anton Cermak.

What vehicle was given the special bullet-proof treatment?
A 1939 Lincoln.

What was this vehicle popularly called?

The Sunshine Special.

King Alfonso XIII of Spain was a great auto enthusiast and actually drove in competition. He set a speed record in the 1912 San Sebastian to Madrid race and even allowed his name to be used for a high-performance car. What was the company that produced it?
Hispano-Suiza. The model was the T-15 sports racer.

Edward VII was the first British monarch to purchase a car. The year was 1900. Was his choice a Rolls-Royce, a Daimler or a Panhard?
A Daimler.

This ex-sportswriter, fight promoter and car salesman found himself with nine unsaleable Thomas Flyers on his hands in 1910, so he started a livery service with them. When even that business got slow, he sent them out onto the streets of Chicago as taxis

The license plate indicates that this vehicle was used for President Truman's inaugural. He inherited it from FDR.

and founded a whole new business. Who was he? Clue: he painted the cars bright yellow.
John B. Hertz.

Match these factory cities with the correct makes:

Indianapolis IN	Tudhope
Elizabeth, NJ	Marmon
Orillia, ON	Durant

From the top: Marmon, Durant and Tudhope.

What was the first car to be driven on the streets of Detroit?
The 1896 King. The vehicle was built by Charles Brady King, who later formed the King Motor Car Company but lost interest in automobiles and turned his attention to aircraft engines after 1916.

What car was James Dean driving when he met his death?
A Porsche 550 Spyder.

What states use(d) these license plate slogans?
Aloha State
Sportsmen's Paradise
The Peach State
From the top: Hawaii, Louisiana, and Georgia.

What country is signified by the international registration GBY?
Malta.

Although few people could be persuaded to use them, what year were seatbelts made mandatory in U.S. cars: 1964, 1968, or 1972?
1964.

A "royal" Spanish sports car.

AUTOMANIA

Princess Grace of Monaco was killed in a car accident in 1982. What was the make of the car: a Rolls-Royce, a Citröen, or a Rover?
A Rover 3500.

Who was driving at the time?
Princess Grace.

Who survived the crash?
Princess Stephanie.

What country is signified by the international registration FL?
Liechtenstein.

Like "chauffeur", much of our automobile lexicon is French. What, for example, is the derivation of "limousine"?
A limousine is a fully enclosed car (except, sometimes, for the chauffeur) that provided complete protection from the elements. The name comes from the protective cloak worn by shepherds in the Limousin district of France.

What is the derivation of "boulevard"?
Also bul-vark (Dutch) or bulwark (English), meaning a rampart for defense. The original boulevards of Paris were simply the line of fortifications around the city.

In the 1970s, "CB" (trucker's) language came into popular usage. Can you match up these terms with their translations?

A pregnant roller skate	A traffic court that fines everybody
Smokey with ears	The accelarator
A Kenosha Cadillac	Police listening in on the CB
A hammer	A VW Beetle
A train station	Any American Motors car

Nash introduced the Metropolitan in 1954 (1956 model shown). Who built it?
Austin of England.

THE CAR IN CULTURE

From the top: a VW Beetle; police listening in on the CB; any American Motors car; the accelerator; a traffic court that fines everybody.

How about these ones?

Green stamps	A weigh station for trucks
Shake the leaves	Dollars
Two-wheeler	Get police out of hiding
Wrapper	Motorcycle
Chicken coop	The colour of a vehicle

From the top: dollars; get police out of hiding; motorcycle; the colour of a vehicle; a weigh station for trucks.

And a few more:

A picture taker	A police car
Bodaceous	Passengers in a car
Seat covers	The last vehicle in a convoy
Tijuana taxi	A police radar unit
The back door	A good, clear signal

From the top: a police radar unit; a good, clear signal; passengers in a car; a police car; the last vehicle in a convoy.

License plates are made in prisons; but what state actually said "Prison Made" on theirs?
Montana.

What do these initials stand for?
NADA
EPA
GPDA
From the top: National Automotive Dealers' Association, Environmental Protection Association, and Grand Prix Drivers' Association.

What states use(d) these license plate slogans?
Vacationland
The Wheat State
The Treasure State
From the top: Maine, Kansas, and Montana.

What U.S. President's daughter owned a Chevrolet Corvair? Clue: it was a 1963 model.
Lucy Baines Johnson.

Why couldn't Ford market the 1964 Mercury Comet "Caliente" in Mexico?
Because "Caliente" is street slang in Mexico for a "lady of the night".

What country is signified by the international registration BR?
Brazil.

This British car gave rise to a name in women's fashions in the sixties. What was the fashion?
The Mini skirt.

The car population has grown steadily since the turn of the century. How many cars are currently in service worldwide: 250 million, 320 million, or 400 million?
Approximately 400 million.

What is the car population of the United States: 116 million, 138 million, or 144 million?
About 144 million.

That represents one passenger car for every 1.8 people. What is the ratio in Canada: 1.5, 1.9, or 2.2?
2.2.

AUTOMANIA

What is the ratio in the USSR: 12.0, 21.3, or 24.0?
24 people per car.

And in China?
1,374 Chinese per car.

It was known as "Vehicle City" in 1901, but it wasn't Detroit.
Flint, Michigan was the home of America's biggest carriage maker, Durant-Dort and several other carriage and wagon companies.

What was the unusual purchase plan devised for buyers of the KDF Wagen (VW Beetle)?
Prospective buyers were provided with books into which they could affix 'trading stamps' and thereby build up credit towards the full purchase price.

Whose idea was it?
It is attributed to Adolf Hitler.

How many purchases were made in this manner?
None. WWII intervened before the 'People's Car' could go into production.

The 4-CV model launched in 1947, put Renault back in business after WWII, but why were all the vehicles painted 'Desert Sand Yellow'?
Paint was hard to get in post-war Europe. But Renault was able to secure a bulk order of paint that had been left over from Field Marshall Rommel's Afrika Korps.

Zsa Zsa Gabor was jailed for three days last year for slugging a cop who had noticed her expired licence plate. What was she driving?
A Rolls-Royce

What was unusual about the Dale 3-wheeler "economy commuter" introduced to potential investors in California by Elizabeth Carmichael in 1975?
It was phony. It had no engine, transmission or running gear.

What was unusual about Liz Carmichael?
She was a man. Jerry Dean Michael was subsequently arrested and charged with fraud.

CHAPTER 6 🏷 THE ADVERTISED CAR

In the beginning, the automobile was news — just by being. The pioneers, faced with a doubting and sometimes hostile public, turned to durability trials, record runs and races to prove that the automobile was to be taken seriously. And the racing generated publicity, putting names like Peugeot, Ford, Thomas, Daimler, Renault and Mercedes into the public consciousness.

But with the growth of the industry came the need to compete for the customer's attention, and automotive advertising appeared. Blunt and simple at first, it displayed the subtlety of a sledgehammer. In a 1905 advertisement Ford said "Don't Experiment — Just Buy A Ford". Perhaps it was in response to this that REO proclaimed, "Get The Real Thing!" Studebaker, on the other hand made a veiled sally at the snob in everyone by proclaiming the 1908 Suburban "A Necessary Adjunct to Every Suburban Or Country Home". Come to think of it, nothing much has changed.

"Ask The Man Who Owns One" is the longest running — and perhaps best known — advertising slogan ever written. What car did it promote: Studebaker, Packard, or Cadillac?
Packard.

How long was it in use: 23, 41, or 55 years?
A total of 55 years, from 1901 to 1956.

The 1948 Tucker Torpedo sank without trace, not the victim of "The Big Three", but simply because of inadequate financing and poor management.

AUTOMANIA

Who was responsible for these advertising slogans?
Think Small
There's a _____ in Your Future
Oh! What a Feeling
From the top: Volkswagen, Ford, and Toyota.

What company used the ghostly names "Phantom" and "Wraith" for their cars?
Rolls-Royce

What do the four rings of Audi symbolize?
They were the symbol of Auto-Union, the company formed in 1932 by the merger of Horch, Wanderer, DKW and Audi.

What actor do you associate with "...rich Corinthian leather"?
Ricardo Montalban.

What company was Ricardo talking about?
Chrysler.

George C. Scott had never done a TV commercial before he stood up for this maker. Was it Audi of America, Renault, or American Motors?
American Motors. He was promoting AMC's Renault-based cars.

How much did Scott earn for doing these commercials?
An estimated one million dollars (U.S.).

What company has used the slogan "The Best Car in the World"?
Rolls-Royce

What automobile manufacturer's name is Latin for "I roll"?
Volvo.

What famous flyer did Hudson invite to christen the new 1932 Essex Terraplane. Was it Eddie Rickenbacker, Wiley Post, or Amelia Earhart?
Amelia Earhart.

What do these famous initials stand for?
BSA
BMW
NSU
Bayerische Motoren Werke, and Neckarsulmer Strickmaschinen Union.

When General Motors introduced the Beretta in 1987, they were unknowingly infringing on someone else's brand name. What was the other company?
The Italian gunmaker, Beretta.

Beretta, the gunmaker, sued GM for $250,000,000. What was the outcome?
When the lawyers had finished, GM agreed to pay the Beretta Foundation for Cancer Research half a million dollars, and legal costs.

What sixties TV songstress exhorted us to "See the U.S.A. in Your Chevrolet"?
Dinah Shore.

What companies used these 'macho' numbers?
Z-28
Boss 302
440 Magnum
From the top: Chevrolet Camaro, Mustang, and Dodge.

What is the name of the Michelin Tire Man?
Monsieur Bibendum.

THE ADVERTISED CAR

Complete this slogan: "Baseball, Hot Dogs, Apple Pie and ..."
Chevrolet.

What cars were billed as "Lion-Hearted" in 1954 ads?
Chrysler.

What companies advertised these models?
_____ Flaminia
_____ Zodiac
_____ Polara
From the top: Lancia, Ford (Great Britain), and Dodge.

Who was the "Sheriff of Scat City" in these 1970s car commercials?
Joe Higgins.

Whose commercials were they: Mercury, Dodge, or American Motors?
Dodge.

What company used the cartoon characters "Wile E. Coyote" and "Beep-beep Roadrunner" in its TV ads?
Plymouth.

In Porsche Carrera, what does "Carrera" mean?
It is Spanish for "race".

Colourful character. What tire company created a logo depicting a very gentlemanly rhinoceros?
The Armstrong Rubber Company.

What oil company claimed it was "Best in the Long Run".
Marathon.

What was the correct name for Plymouth's "Beep-beep Roadrunner"?
Acceleratti Rapidus Maximus.

The car is the 1932 version of the Essex Terraplane. Who is the lady?
Aviatrix Amelia Earhart.

AUTOMANIA

Dustin Hoffman was the spokesperson for this 1964 import. Was it Fiat, Volkswagen, or Alfa Romeo?
1964 VW Fastback.

These special colours were created in the sixties for a special model. Can you complete the palette?

Anti-Establish	_____
Hulla	_____
Freudian	_____
Thanks	_____
Original	_____

From the top: Mint, Blue, Gilt, Vermillion, and Cinnamon.

What was the make and model car which offered these colours?
Ford Maverick.

What company's slogan is "Sturdy — Stylish — Swedish"?
SAAB.

In 1957 it was billed as "America's Most Powerful Car", with 375 h.p. What was it?
The Chrysler 300C.

The ad men had to give automatic transmissions names that implied

The Michelin Tire man has been around since the turn of the century. According to this 1908 brochure, "Michelin drinks obstacles!"

power and smoothness. It had to sound better than the other guy's. Try to match these trannies to the correct makers:

Drive-Master	Buick
Hydra-Matic	Chrysler
Powerglide	Hudson
Torqueflite	Cadillac
Triple Turbine	Chevrolet
Transmission	

From the top: Hudson, Cadillac, Chevrolet, Chrysler, and Buick.

What tire company developed the "Tiger Paws" mascot?
Uniroyal.

The Datsun 240Z was called what in Japan?
Fairlady Z.

Can you name the sponsors of these famous, long-running TV shows?
Bonanza
Maverick
Dragnet
From the top: Chevrolet, Jeep (Kaiser-Jeep), and Ford.

What American car company used a coat of arms with the French motto, "Je Suis Prêt" (I am ready)? Was it Duesenburg, Lincoln, or Frazer?
Frazer.

What company logo depicted a swallow in flight: DKW, Austin, or Simca?
Simca.

What company logo depicts a six-star constellation? Clue: it's Japanese.
Subaru.

Typical artwork by coachbuilder Saoutchik to advertise a glamorous body. For what car?
A 1930 Cord Town Car.

AUTOMANIA

What does it all mean? Car companies like to embellish car names with add-on letters and numbers. Sometimes it means something. What about these?
Pontiac GTO
The "H" in Shelby GT-350H
Dodge R/T
From the top: Gran Turismo Omologato;

"Hertz" — it was the special model offered by the rental company; Road and Track.

See if you can match up the gas stations with their high-octane products:

Gulf	Red Crown
Phillips	Super No-Nox

What they did to get attention. This little balancing act was to demonstrate the smooth and steady ride of the 1902 Curved Dash Oldsmobile.

THE ADVERTISED CAR

Standard   Sky Chief
Texaco   Flite Fuel
From the top: Super No-Nox, Flite Fuel, Red Crown, and Sky Chief.

What car manufacturer sponsored the first Disneyland TV shows? Was it Dodge, Nash, or Studebaker?
Nash (later American Motors when Nash-Kelvinator and Hudson merged).

Push-button gear selectors were all the rage once. Who made these ones?
Teletouch
Magic Touch
Keyboard
From the top: Edsel, Mercury, and De Soto.

The emblem of this U.S. sports car company shows winged Pegasus flying through the capital letter "A". What is the company?
Arnolt-Bristol.

What company was brave enough to promote this tongue-twister in 1965: "Twin-Stick Floor Shift with Instant Overtake"?
Rambler. It referred to a transmission with 5 forward speeds.

What car company identified different models with letters of the Greek alphabet, as in Alpha, Gamma, Lambda etc.? Clue: it's Italian.
Lancia.

What car company symbol depicts the profile of a twin-engined plane head-on? Clue: the company also builds aircraft.
SAAB.

Proof that if you give something an "extinct" name, it may soon follow suit. The 1953 Kaiser Dragon with extinct upholstery.

AUTOMANIA

What company advertised Dinosaur Vinyl upholstery for this 1952 model? Was it Kaiser, Hudson, or Crosley?
Kaiser, for the Dragon model.

What was Linda Vaughn better known as?
Miss Hurst Golden Shifter.

In 1983, Renault introduced this fiery sports coupe to its American Motors dealers. It didn't catch fire. What was it?
The Fuego (Spanish for "fire").

The Ford slogan "It's What's up Front That Counts" was coined for a specific, high-performance model. What was it?
The Ford Shelby 350 GT.

Why were Bentleys banned from exhibiting at the 1930 French Auto Show?
Woolf Barnato, one of the Le Mans-winning "Bentley Boys", raced the famous "Blue Train" from Nice to London, and beat it by four hours. The French were not amused.

What was better known as "The Judge"?
The Pontiac GTO.

What was better known as "The Rebel Machine"?
The 1969 American Motors Rebel with a 390 CID V-8.

What companies used these slogans?
A Car You Can Believe In.
We Are Driven!
Safety Fast.
From the top: Volvo, Datsun (now Nissan), and MG.

What Japanese company name means "Fifty Bells"?
Isuzu.

What Japanese company name means "Three Diamonds"?
Mitsubishi.

In the fifties and sixties, automotive advertising copywriters were out of control. Like fins and chrome, there was no excess that was not pursued. See if you can match these "auto-hyperboles" with the guilty vehicle:
Jetaway Hydra-Matic Drive   1950 Chevrolet
Miracle H-Power   1953 Olds "98"
Unitized Knee-   1951 Hudson
Action Ride
From the top: Olds "98", Hudson Hornet, and Chevrolet.

And what about these?
Velvet Pressure
Jumbo Drum
Brakes   1952 Nash
Touch-O-Matic   1953 Chevrolet
Overdrive   1952 Mercury
Road Guide
Fenders
From the top: Chevrolet, Mercury, and Nash.

Everyone has heard of the "Green Berets". Where would you find the "Blue Berets"?
In an "Airstream" caravan. More correctly, any member of the Wally Byam Caravan Club International.

The name Scania belongs with what car company name?
SAAB.

THE ADVERTISED CAR

Who hired the Eiffel Tower to advertise his company name: Renault, Bugatti, or Citröen?
Citröen.

The one hundred foot high Citröen logo, emblazoned in electric lights, was a Parisian fixture for one, six or nine years?
Nine years — from 1926 to 1934 — much to the annoyance of Louis Renault.

What is the meaning of the Volvo emblem?
It is the old chemical symbol for iron.

Fashion designers were sometimes brought in to "hype" interiors. What is the make and model of this Gucci effort?
1972 Hornet Sportabout.

Although Chrysler's Airflow model was doomed to a very short life, it was built and marketed in Britain for a short time. What name was it given in that market?
The Heston.

What company used the slogan "Grace, Pace and Space"?
Jaguar.

What was "The Car That Made Good in a Day"? Stutz, Cord, or Duesenburg?
Completed only two weeks before the event, Stutz entered their first car in the 1911 Indianapolis 500. It finished 11th, which was, apparently, justification for the advertising slogan!

AUTOMANIA

The original Buick Skylark of 1953 was a "limited edition" only. What would you find printed on the steering wheel hub?
The signature of the owner, cast in a lucite medallion.

What companies sponsored these long-running TV shows?
Lawrence Welk
Mr. Ed
Howdy Doody Show
From the top: Dodge, Studebaker, and Edsel.

What company used the "Tree of Knowledge" symbol in the thirties?
Chrysler.

What do these add-on initials mean?
Camaro RS

Buick GS
Shelby GT-350 KR
From the top: Rally Sport, Gran Sport, and King of the Road.

Match these high-octane brands with the right gas stations:

Sinclair	Super 5D
Atlantic	Power X
Cities Service	Boron
DX	Imperial

From the top: Power X, Imperial, Super 5D, and Boron.

What company offered a pickup called "L'il Hustler"?
Datsun.

These stars lent their status to help promote certain cars. Match the stars

The pride of the Marines stands in front of his 1926 Packard 326. Who is he?
Gene Tunney, World Heavyweight Boxing Champion.

THE ADVERTISED CAR

with the cars:

Jack Dempsey — 1936 Dodge
Bob Hope — 1938 De Soto
Shirley Temple — 1937 Studebaker

From the top: De Soto, Studebaker, and Dodge.

What oil company developed a gargoyle mascot?
Mobil Oil.

"Power Brute" was a gorilla-on-wheels mascot developed by what auto supplier company?
Borg-Warner.

What companies attracted us with these creatures?

_____ Cougar
_____ Gazelle
_____ Lark

From the top: Mercury, Singer, and Studebaker.

Since his retirement, Jackie Stewart has been a spokesman for what car company?
The Ford Motor Company.

Complete these "specialist" car names:

_____ Plus Four
_____ Stingray
_____ Cimarron

From the top: Morgan, Corvette, and Cadillac.

George Mason, president of Nash-Kelvinator, got into conversation with this English sports car builder on a trans-Atlantic voyage in 1950. The result was a sporty two-seater that Nash showed in February 1951. Who was the English sports car builder?
Donald Healey.

What was the vehicle he and Mason introduced?
The Nash-Healey.

Pinin Farina and AMC President George Mason (at the wheel), pulled off this wonderful sports car, before Corvette or Thunderbird, perhaps a little too soon for the market.

Rebodied in 1952 by Pinin Farina, the Nash-Healey remained in production only one, three, or five years?
Three.

Who coined the phrase "56 for '56" and what did it mean?
Lee Iacocca. As Sales Manager for Ford's Philadelphia District, he reasoned that customers should be able to buy a 1956 Ford with a modest (20%) downpayment, and monthly payments of $56. It worked.

One of the most famous "break-through" advertisements appeared in 1923. It read, "Somewhere West of Laramie...there's a bronco-busting, steer-roping girl who knows what I'm talking about..." What car was being advertised?
The Jordan Playboy.

Published in 1915, "The Penalty of Leadership" is considered by some to be one of the best-written automotive

The advertisement that changed copywriting from "nuts and bolts" to "imagery".

Somewhere West of Laramie

SOMEWHERE west of Laramie there's a broncho-busting, steer-roping girl who knows what I'm talking about.

She can tell what a sassy pony, that's a cross between greased lightning and the place where it hits, can do with eleven hundred pounds of steel and action when he's going high, wide and handsome.

The truth is—the Playboy was built for her.

Built for the lass whose face is brown with the sun when the day is done of revel and romp and race.

She loves the cross of the wild and the tame.

There's a savor of links about that car—of laughter and lilt and light—a hint of old loves—and saddle and quirt. It's a brawny thing—yet a graceful thing for the sweep o' the Avenue.

Step into the Playboy when the hour grows dull with things gone dead and stale.

Then start for the land of real living with the spirit of the lass who rides, lean and rangy, into the red horizon of a Wyoming twilight.

JORDAN

ads of all time. What company did it represent?
Cadillac.

What car company is currently (1989) "Changing the Landscape"?
Chrysler.

Match these stars to their cars:
Ted Williams   1962 Ford Falcon
Charlie Brown   1937 Nash
and Snoopy   Ambassador
                       1951 Dodge
Babe Ruth
From the top: Dodge, Ford Falcon, and Nash Ambassador.

What car companies do you associate with these spokesmen?
Jim Garner
Dan Gurney
John Houseman
From the top: Mazda, Toyota, and Chrysler.

Who or what is "Mr. Goodwrench"?
The parts division of General Motors.

Which tire company should you consider "Because so much is riding on your tires..."?
Michelin.

"Who Could Ask for Anything More!" was the campaign heading for what company?
Toyota.

These slogans were attached to specific models. See if you can match them up:
The Great
Imposter   1964 Oldsmobile
Where The Action
Is   1963 Ford Galaxie
Ten Million Dollar
Ride   1967 Tempest OHC
From the top: Tempest, Olds, and Ford.

Chrysler did it "his way" in this 1982 Imperial.

AUTOMANIA

What company declared "When Better Cars Are Built (We) Will Build Them"?
Buick.

About what car was it claimed "At 60 mph, all you can hear is the clock!"?
Rolls-Royce.

In Porsche 911E, what does the "E" stand for?
Einspritzung (fuel injection).

In 1982 Frank Sinatra did some work for this company and, in recognition, they named a model The Frank Sinatra Edition. What was the company?
Chrysler; it was an Imperial.

In 1930 this company introduced "Free Motoring". For the first year — or 7,500 miles — the owner got free gas, oil and maintenance. It didn't help; the company was re-structured as American Bantam in 1934. What was the company?
American Austin Co.

Who combined their 1953 car ads with expensive jewellery from Harry Winston and Van Cleef and Arpels?
Cadillac.

More great words from the ad copywriters. Match them to the culprits:
Vacamatic   Ford
Flightomatic   Chrysler
Cruise-O-Matic   Studebaker
From the top: Chrysler, Studebaker, and Ford.

Who sponsored Paul Whiteman's "TV Teen Club" in the fifties?
Nash-Kelvinator.

Good move. In 1956 the Dual Motors Corporation decided to change the name of this car to Dual-Ghia. What

On second thoughts, let's call it the Dual-Ghia.

THE ADVERTISED CAR

was it before?
The Firebomb.

This company was famous for its highway signs. They featured a series of doggerel verses on successive billboards. What was the company?
Burma-Shave.

Who said, "If you can find a better built, better backed car — buy it!"
Lee Iacocca.

"Mean Mary Jean" appeared in 1960s TV commercials for what company?
Plymouth.

The car characterized as "...a living room on wheels" was first used in product brochures from Ford, Chrysler, or Hudson?
1949 Ford brochures.

"Thriftmaster", "Loadmaster", and "Jobmaster" were all engine names applied to what company's trucks in the fifties?
Chevrolet.

What company advertised "Wide Stance Chassis" in 1957?
Oldsmobile.

My Farewell Car

By R. E. Olds, Designer

Reo the Fifth — the car I now bring out — is regarded by me as close to finality. Embodied here are the final results of my 25 years of experience. I do not believe that a car materially better will ever be built. In any event, this car marks my limit. So I've called it My Farewell Car.

My 24th Model

This is the twenty-fourth model which I have created in the past 25 years.

They have run from one to six cylinders — from 6 to 60 horsepower. From the primitive cars of the early days to the most luxurious modern machines.

I have run the whole gamut of automobile experience. I have learned the right and the wrong from tens of thousands of users.

In this Farewell car I adopt the size which has come to be standard — the 30 to 35 horsepower, 4-cylinder car.

Where It Excels

The best I have learned in 25 years is the folly of taking chances. So the chiefest point where this car excels is in excess of care and caution.

In every steel part I use the best alloy ever proved out for the purpose. And all my steel is analyzed, to prove its accord with the formula.

I test my gears with a crushing machine — not a hammer. Thus I know to exactness what each gear will stand.

I put the magneto to a radical test. The carburetor is doubly heated, for low-grade gasoline.

I use Nickel Steel axles of unusual size, with Timken roller bearings. I use Vanadium Steel connections.

So in every part. Each device and material is the best known for the purpose. The margin of safety is always extreme.

In Finish, Too

I have also learned that people like stunning appearance. So my body finish consists of 17 coats. The upholstering is deep, and of hair-filled, genuine leather. The lamps are enameled, as per the latest vogue. Even the engine is nickel-trimmed.

The wheel base is long — the tonneau is roomy — the wheels are large — the car is over-tired. In every part of the car you'll find the best that is possible — and more than you expect.

Reo the Fifth
$1,055

30-35
Horsepower

Wheel Base—
112 Inches

Wheels—
34 Inches

Demountable
Rims

Speed—
45 Miles per
Hour

Made with
2, 4 and 5
Passenger
Bodies

Ransom Olds still had twenty-four years to go when he announced his "Farewell Car".

It was billed as "My Farewell Car". The maker's advertisement said, "After 25 years, after creating 24 models and building tens of thousands of cars — here's the best I know!" Who said it: Henry Ford, Frank Duryea, or Ransom Olds?
Ransom Eli Olds.

What car was he referring to?
The REO of 1912, but it wasn't the last. REO stayed around until 1936.

What prestigious British car company would not publicize its horsepower, but simply answered "Enough", when asked for the rating?
Rolls-Royce.

In 1964 the PRNDL stick was formally recognized by the industry. What was it?
The automatic gearshift: Park, Reverse, Neutral, Drive and Low.

After 112 years in production, Studebaker closed down its U.S. facilities in 1963 and moved. Where did it go to?
Ontario, Canada.

This vehicle, introduced in 1931, was named for Notre Dame's famous football coach. What was it?
The Rockne.

What company made it?
Studebaker. It was discontinued in 1933 following Rockne's death in a plane accident.

This is what the ad manager at Thermos came up with in 1910.

CHAPTER 7 ✦ THE CAR IN WAR

Insofar as the automobile replaced the horse, it also replaced the cavalry and military transportation in general. Not right away, of course, because old ideas — particularly old military ideas — are slow to change. But the real contribution of the automotive industry in time of war is not so much vehicles as it is engineering capacity. Planes, aero engines, dirigibles, even ships, have all rolled out of automotive plants at one time or another.

For example, in World War I, more than 50% of Allied aircraft were powered by this engine developed by Swiss automobile engineer Marc Birkigt. What was the engine?
The Hispano-Suiza engine, much-loved by Spad and Nieuport fighter pilots.

In World War II, the Merlin engine powered such diverse aircraft as the Spitfire, Mustang, Lancaster bomber and Mosquito. What automobile maker designed it?
Rolls-Royce.

The need for Merlins was critical in the early days of the war. Britain sought help from Henry Ford, who refused to build any. What company took on the task: Studebaker, General Motors, or Packard?
Packard.

Henry later changed his mind and more than 34,000 Merlin engines were built at a "shadow factory" near Manchester, England. How did the Germans help in setting up the factory?
Jig-boring machines had to be imported from Switzerland. That meant allowing them to be shipped through German-occupied France. The Germans cooperated because

they needed light machine tools from Switzerland too!

In May of 1942, Ford's Willow Run, Michigan plant opened — but not for the production of cars. What was to be built there?
Henry Ford was going to apply automotive manufacturing techniques to aircraft production. The plane to be built was the B-24 Liberator.

In Germany, the Blitzkreig was spearheaded by the finest tanks in the world at that time. They were the product of Mercedes-Benz, VW, or Porsche?
Dr. Ferdinand Porsche was the designer of the Panzer tanks.

Where did the Jeep first see action in WWI: Guadalcanal, The Phillipines, or North Africa?
North Africa, with the Allied forces fighting General Rommel and his Afrika Korp. This was several months before Pearl Harbour.

Who created the Jeep: Willys, Bantam, or Ford?
All three made contributions, but in competitive testing carried out by the Quartermaster Depot during the winter of 1940–41, it was the Willys that won out.

How did the Jeep get its name?
It has become generally accepted that it is a contraction of the letters GP, meaning General Purpose. However, the GP designation was never given to the Jeep. On the other hand, there was an animal character in the Popeye comic strip of the time — Eugene the Jeep — "which was neither fowl nor beast, but knew all the answers and could do most anything." We may never know for sure.

What were the Chigger, Peep, Leapin' Leana, Blitz-Buggy and Puddle-Jumper?
They were all names applied to the Jeep before the final name stuck.

The three Jeep prototypes presented to the Quartermaster Depot had names. Match the prototype names to the companies.

Quad   Ford
BRC   Willys
Pygmy   Bantam

From the top: Willys, Bantam, and Ford.

Willys won the army contract but couldn't provide the massive numbers required. What company did it licence to produce the Jeep: Ford, Bantam, or General Motors?
Ford. By war's end, Willys had produced some 360,000 Jeep (MB) models and Ford produced some 278,000 Jeep (GPW) models. Bantam had to be content with some contracts for Jeep trailers and other ancillary equipment.

What was the German equivalent of the Jeep?
The Kubelwagen.

Who made it?
It was designed by Ferdinand Porsche for Volkswagen.

What was the amphibious version of the Kubelwagen called?
The Schwimmwagen.

What was the Red Ball Express?
The U.S. Army's transport operation in WWII

The "Quad". This was the winning Willys prototype in the contest for what turned out to be the "Jeep" contract.

that kept the Allied Forces supplied in Europe.

What car was General George S. Patton riding in when he had his fatal accident: a Jeep, a Cadillac, or a Packard?
It was a 1939 Cadillac, one of 15 assembled from parts in France.

The only way to halt the German advance on Paris in 1914 was by rapidly moving troops in counter-attack. But there was no transport. How did General Gallieni solve the problem?
He called a cab, or rather, 1,300 Renault 8CV taxicabs, and had them move the troops to the front. They became the famous "Taxis of Marne".

Who said: "A Rolls in the desert is like rubies"? Clue: he was leading the Arab Revolt in WWI.
T. E. Lawrence ("Lawrence of Arabia").

British "Tommies" in WWI were impressed with these American trucks. They thought they were tough as bulldogs, and called them that. The company liked the idea and made the bulldog its emblem. What is the company?
Mack.

This "Peace Ship" was sent to Europe at the beginning of WWI packed with intellectuals and other celebrities. Their objective was to bring about peace by "continuous mediation". What was the name of the ship?
The Oscar II.

This Rolls-Royce armored car is camouflaged for use in the WWI German East African Campaign. Note the open radiator doors.

Who sponsored the expedition: Henry Leland, William Durant, or Henry Ford?
Henry Ford. It didn't work.

Who invented the tank?
In 1914 Winston Churchill suggested that vehicles with caterpillar tracks could overcome the problems of trench warfare. Ignored by the War Office, he was able to persuade Major Hetherington of the Dunkirk Naval Armoured Car Squadron to work on some prototypes.

How did the "tank" get its name?
In World War I, the British began the development of a secret weapon that could end the stalemate of trench warfare. For security purposes it was code-named "Water-carrier". However, the military mania for acronyms turned this into "W.C." which was considered too rude ("W.C." means water closet or toilet). And so to avoid vulgarity, "Water-carrier" became "Tank", and so it has remained.

The Saladin, Saracen and Stalwart are all armoured vehicles designed by this British company. Is it Austin, Rolls-Royce, or Alvis?
Alvis. Rolls-Royce provides the power.

Captain Robert G. Howie developed this machine gun carrier in 1936. What was it called?
The Howie "Belly-Flopper".

When Barney Roos of Willys named his Jeep prototype the "Quad", he was making a historical reference. What vehicle was he referring to?
The Jeffery Quad truck of WWI.

What were the unique features of the Jeffery Quad?
It had 4WD, four-wheel brakes and steered with all four wheels! It also had driving positions at both ends of the vehicle. It was the first of the completely armored trucks used by the U.S. and Canadian military of 1915.

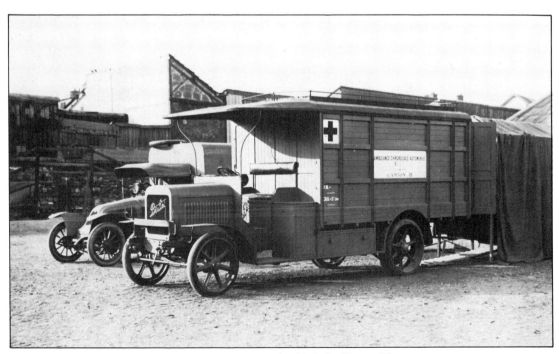

This French Berliet ambulance and Schneider car represent what kind of military unit?
A WWI M.A.S.H. unit.

THE CAR IN WAR

Where were the Jeffery Quads first used in a military action? In the Phillipines, on the Mexican border, or in France?
General "Black" Jack Pershing used them against Pancho Villa on the Mexican border.

Pershing was given a Type 57 Cadillac in 1919 by the employees at Cadillac. What was unique about this car?
Every part was stamped with the U.S. flag.

What U.S. company began mass production of tanks in 1941?
Chrysler.

What was the model of the tank?
MK. III General Grant.

Field Marshall Montgomery's staff car was dubbed "Old Faithful" and saw service in North Africa and Europe. What was it: a 1940 Daimler, a 1941 Humber Super Snipe, or a 1938 Armstrong-Siddeley?
A 1941 Humber Super Snipe.

What was Adolf Hitler's preferred staff car: Mercedes-Benz, Horch, or Opel?
Mercedes-Benz.

What are "caissons"?
Ammunition wagons.

What was the DUKW?
Fondly known as the "Duck", it was the six-wheeled amphibious vehicle developed in WWII by General Motors.

A WWI British "tank" in need of service after the Battle of Cambrai.

He first used these 4 × 4 trucks in action against Pancho Villa on the Mexican/U.S. border, then in WWI. Who is he?
General "Black Jack" Pershing.

THE CAR IN WAR

This 1910 "anti-aircraft" unit was mounted on a pretty expensive set of wheels. Can you identify the car? *It's a Cadillac.*

This Jeep convoy is crossing a Burmese river. Who is the officer in the cavalry hat? *General "Vinegar Joe" Stillwell, commander of Chinese troops in WWII.*

While it is impossible to name the inventor of the automobile, there has never been a lack of contenders, and the same applies to many of the automotive milestones since then. Inventors and engineers, by their very nature, tend to be secretive, eccentric and jealous, and some have even been known to fudge the dates here and there if it meant getting an edge on the competition. The fact that there is so much room for argument just makes it all the more fascinating.

Because his son complained about the hard, uncomfortable ride on his tricycle, Scots veterinary surgeon William Boyd Dunlop was inspired to invent the first pneumatic tire in 1888. An instant success, it launched a whole new industry. But who actually introduced the first pneumatic tire for automobiles: Dunlop, Michelin, or Pirelli?
Michelin, in 1895. They introduced the tires at the Paris-Bordeaux race and retired their entry due to too many flats.

The first front-wheel drive production car was introduced by Peugeot, Alvis, or Cord?
Cord in 1929.

What was the model?
The L29.

The electric self-starter was introduced in 1908, 1911, or 1920?
1911.

Who was the inventor?
Charles F. Kettering of DELCO.

What did the letters DELCO signify?
Dayton Engineering Laboratories Co.

First of its kind: the classic Cord L-29 of 1929.

AUTOMANIA

What vehicle featured the first electric starter: Ford, Packard, or Cadillac?
The 1911 Cadillac. The following year, Cadillac models featured the starter and an independent electrical system, the first on a production car.

What award did Cadillac win for this innovation?
The RAC Dewar Trophy.

What do the letters RAC stand for?
The Royal Automobile Club (Great Britain).

The Royal Automobile Club of Britain established the Dewar Trophy to recognize outstanding automotive advances. It was won for the first time by an American company in 1908. Which company was it: Buick, Cadillac or Winton?
Cadillac.

Why was the 1908 Dewar Trophy awarded to Cadillac?
Three Cadillacs were disassembled and all the parts were mixed up. Three vehicles

Cadillac was awarded the RAC's Dewar Trophy in 1909 for demonstrating "the inter-changeability of parts". Wilfred C. Leland, Jr., grandson of Henry Leland, here demonstrates the capacity of the Dewar Trophy.

were then rebuilt, using all the parts and the vehicles were successfully driven off. This demonstrated the interchangeability of parts for the first time, an essential ingredient in mass production.

What classic car radiator was designed to resemble a racing horseshoe?
Bugatti.

What do Champion Spark Plugs and AC Spark Plugs have in common?
Frenchman Albert Champion founded the company bearing his name. However, in 1908, William Durant attempted to acquire the company. When he was turned down, he simply hired Albert away from Champion Spark Plugs and formed a rival company using Albert's initials!

The American Motors Pacer, introduced in 1975, featured the 4.2 litre, inline six. But it wasn't meant to. What kind of engine was the vehicle designed around?
A rotary engine.

The engine was to be a joint venture between AMC and another manufacturer. Was it Volkswagen, Renault, or GM?
GM. The engine was aborted prior to the Pacer introduction.

The Society of Automobile Engineers was formed in 1905 and then changed its name in 1917. What was the new name?
The Society of Automotive Engineers (SAE).

After Pierce-Arrow folded in 1938, what company continued to use their V-8 and V-12 engines for the next 20 years.
Seagrave, to power its fire engines.

William Stout, famous for his design of the Fort Trimotor plane, tried his hand at an innovative vehicle design in 1935. Featuring a rear-engine and rear drive, the design presages today's minivans. What was it called?
The Scarab.

If it looks like a beetle, call it a beetle. The 1936 Scarab . . . was it the forerunner of today's minivans?

AUTOMANIA

The British MMC model shown at the 1903 Paris Exposition was luxuriously equipped. It featured plush upholstery, folding seats, a speaking tube, and what other unique communications device?
A version of the "ship's telegraph", so that directions could be given to the chauffeur "without actually having to speak to him".

The Lockheed Lightning (P-38) fighter of WWII inspired what automobile design feature?
Fins. Harley Earl of General Motors was the culprit.

What vehicle first featured Harley's fins?
The 1949 Cadillac.

Many early Morgan 3-wheelers were powered by JAP engines. What do the initials signify?
They are the initials of the engine designer J.A. Prestwick.

What is a "Roie de Belges" body?
A style of high-backed bucket seats on an open touring body, so-called because it was designed for King Leopold of Belgium for his 1901 Mercedes.

Harley Earl's fins were so conservative in the beginning.

The oldest photograph in the National Automotive History Collection depicts a veteran of the Civil War with friends, in his favourite 4-in-hand wagon. In 1879, he formed a bicycle company and followed that up with the Columbia Electric Company, making electric powered automobiles. Who was he?
Albert Augustus Pope, founder of the Pope-Toledo, Pope-Hartford and Pope-Waverly car companies.

ENGINEERING & DESIGN

This innovative British designer insisted that the seated motorist should be at the same eye level as a pedestrian. Was it Frederick Lanchester, Henry Royce or John Napier?
Frederick Lanchester.

Giving credit where its due, can you name the great designers behind these classic shapes?

Ferrari GTO   Gordon Beuhrig
Avanti   Pinin Farina
Cord 810   Tom Kellog
From the top: Pinin Farina, Tom Kellog (Raymond Leowy Studios), Gordon Buehrig.

And what about these classics?

Jeep MA   Alec Issigonis
'56 Corvette   Barney Roos
Austin Mini   Bill Mitchell
From the top: Barney Roos, Bill Mitchell, Alec Issigonis.

And who were responsible for these classic marques?

1968 AMX   Harley Earl
1959 Cadillac   Virgil Exner
1955 Chrysler 300 Richard Teague
From the top: Richard Teague, Harley Earl, Virgil Exner

What was the first production car to offer servo-assisted brakes on all four wheels: Jaguar, Rolls-Royce, or Hispano-Suiza?
Hispano-Suiza.

When did it introduce this feature: 1919, 1923, or 1925?
1919. It was such a good design that Rolls-Royce decided to copy it five years later.

What was unusual about the driver's side rear passenger door on the 1949 Kaiser Traveller?
It was welded shut.

What three things did the 1960 Chevrolet Corvair and the VW Beetle have in common?
Air-cooled engine, rear mounted engine, and rear swing axles.

1929 Hispano-Suiza

AUTOMANIA

What do the Mercedes-Benz 300SL, the DeLorean and the Bricklin have in common?
Gull-wing doors.

What does the designation 'CV' stand for, as in Citröen 2-CV?
Cheveaux Vapeur — horsepower.

Looking for a marketing boost, George Mason had the 1952 Nash Statesman and Ambassador models completely re-styled by this Italian designer. Was it Ghia, Bertone, or Pinin Farina?
Pinin Farina.

What are the two unusual features of the 1911 Reeves Octo-Auto?
It had eight wheels, all of which steered the car.

The "honeycomb" radiator, first seen in 1899, became the standard for quality cars for the next thirty years.

What company introduced it?
Daimler, designed by Paul, son of Gottleib Daimler.

Before "electrics" were introduced for lighting, what was the common form of lighting system?
Acetylene, in which water is dripped steadily onto carbide.

What was a "sprag" used for?
An iron spike under the car that could be let down on a steep hill to prevent roll-back.

In 1909 this car was the first to offer brakes on all four wheels as standard. What was the company?
Isotta-Fraschini.

While Cadillac is credited with the first mass-production V-8 engine in 1914, they had been seen before. As early as 1903, Frenchman Clement Ader built a team of V-8 racers and, in 1910, this

Not content with his "Sexto-Auto" of 1911, Mr. Reeves decided to go for eight in 1912 with this "Octo-Auto". The eight wheels also steered the car but, unfortunately, not always in conjunction with one another. Reeves went under shortly after.

company began sustained, but limited, production. Was it Mors, Bugatti, or De Dion?
De Dion.

What do the Eagle Premier, Lotus Esprit and Maserati Bora have in common?
They were all styled by Giorgetto Giugiaro of the Ital Design Studio.

What automotive engineering development is credited to Dr. Felix Wankel?
The rotary engine.

The first vehicle to utilize his invention appeared in 1963. Was it a DKW, a Mazda, or an NSU?
The NSU Spyder. Mazda subsequently did much to make the rotary a viable powerplant.

The first Japanese-built car was the work of Yoshida and Uchiyama. Called the Takuri, it was launched in 1902, 1907, or 1916?
1907. Five years earlier, they had built their first prototype with an American engine.

The world's first jet turbine car was demonstrated on March 8, 1950. Named "Jet I", was it the work of Mercedes, Chrysler, or Rover?
Rover.

What was a "trafficator"?
Before turn signals on cars, "trafficators" were mechanical arms that flipped out from the side of the car to indicate turning intentions.

Who made the first practical application of 4WD on a production passenger car: Subaru, American Motors, or Jensen?
The 1966 Jensen.

First V-8 application was introduced by De Dion in 1910. The 1911 model shown.

AUTOMANIA

Before cars talked. In 1921, Michelin devised an ingenious system to let a motorist know when his tire was about to deflate. What was it?

A tiny gun, complete with lock and cartridges, was triggered as the tire deflated. The sound of the shot advised the driver of the impending flat.

What was the first production car to feature a practical disc brake system: Jensen, Jaguar, or Chrysler?

A form of disc brakes was found on the earliest models by Lanchester and later, the AC of 1919. A 1938 racing Miller also featured a disc brake with a simple pressure plate acting on one side of the disc. The 1949 Chrysler Imperials introduced four-wheel, self-energizing disc brakes, in which two discs were pushed apart to press against the sides of the drum. The first application of the "modern, Dunlop-type" disc brakes was on the Jaguar XK150 of 1953.

When was power-steering first made available on a production automobile: 1949, 1951, or 1953?
1951.

Who offered it: Cadillac, Oldsmobile, or Chrysler?
Chrysler. Cadillac, Olds and Buick caught up the following year.

When was the first power-operated convertible top available: 1934, 1938, or 1939?
1934.

What company offered it: Peugeot, Cord, or Daimler?
Peugeot with its "decapotable electrique".

The first car to offer power-assisted, four-wheel brakes did so in 1919. Was it Cadillac, Hispano-Suiza, or Isotta-Fraschini?
Hispano-Suiza.

The Jensen FF of 1966 pioneered 4-Wheel-Drive and a form of ABS braking.

A V-8 engine was shown by De Dion Bouton in 1910, but when was such an engine offered in a production car: 1912, 1914, or 1916?
1914.

What was the car: Buick, Cadillac, or De Dion?
The Cadillac Type 51.

The first tubeless tires were introduced by Goodrich, Michelin, or Dunlop?
Goodrich, in 1948.

Who developed the "balloon" tire: Goodyear, Dunlop or Firestone?
Firestone.

What car did the balloon tires first appear on?
The Cole, in 1923. The following year they were offered by Chrysler on selected models.

What did the Rover "75" of 1950, the 1915 Briscoe, and the 1946 Tucker Torpedo have in common?
A centrally-mounted "cyclops" headlight. The Tucker Torpedo light also swiveled as the steering wheel turned.

The first retractable headlights were a feature of this 1936 classic. What was it?
The Cord 810.

The 1921 Wills Ste. Claire featured this aid to backing-up. What was it?
Back-up lights.

The first curved windshield — without central divider — was introduced in 1914 by Hudson, Kissel, or Locomobile?
Kissel.

Who is credited with developing the diesel engine?
Dr. Rudolph Diesel.

The first production car with an engine that went around and around, instead of up and down.

AUTOMANIA

The first diesel-engine production passenger car was introduced in 1936. What was it?
The Mercedes-Benz 260D.

The first all-steel-bodied, closed car was introduced in 1924 by this company. Was it Dodge, Hudson, or Ford?
Dodge.

The first drive-in gas station was opened in 1913 in Pittsburgh by Atlantic, Gulf, or Standard Oil?
Gulf.

The first 4-wheel-drive car was produced in Holland by Spyker, Minerva, or Mors?
Spyker.

What year was it introduced: 1905, 1908, or 1912?
1905. However, it did not go into series production.

The first car bearing Walter Chrysler's name appeared in 1922, 1924, or 1927?
1924.

A British Rover with characteristic "cyclops eye".

What company pioneered the use of the synchromesh transmission in 1928: Chrysler, Peerless, or Cadillac?
Cadillac.

The first power windows were introduced with this model in 1948. Were they featured by Lincoln, Rolls-Royce, or Daimler?
British Daimler.

The first ignition-starter key was introduced in 1949 by Chrysler, Ford, or Buick?
Chrysler.

Gasoline fuel-injection was first offered on a production car by this German make in 1954. What was the make and model?
Mercedes-Benz 300SL.

Air-conditioning was first offered by this company as an option in 1938. Who was it? Clue: they were already in the business.
Nash-Kelvinator.

This American company was the first to introduce a production sedan with front-wheel-drive and transverse mounted engine. Who was it?
Chrysler with its 1978 Omni/Horizon.

What company developed the steel-belted radial tire: Goodyear, Firestone, or Michelin?
Michelin.

The "cloverleaf" intersection has become part of our vocabulary. The design was patented in 1916 by Arthur Hale of Maryland. When was the first "cloverleaf" built? Was it 1920, 1925, or 1928?
1928, in Woodbridge, New Jersey.

Lockheed is a name associated with automobile hydraulic systems and aircraft production. It is the name of the founder, but what is odd about it?
Malcolm spelt his name Loughead, but it became phoneticized as Lockheed.

Lockheed's hydraulic brake system was first fitted in 1920 to this production automobile. Was it Marmon, Hupmobile, or Duesenberg?
Duesenberg.

The first production diesel-powered passenger car, introduced in 1936.

Hudson introduced this innovation in 1939 to make the ride a little more comfortable. What was it?
Foam rubber cushions for the seats.

In 1925 uniform markings were formalized for U.S. highways built with Federal funding. How were odd and even numbers assigned to highways?
Even numbers were assigned to East-West routes; odd numbers to North-South routes.

1940 saw the general acceptance of this type of headlight. What was it?
The Sealed Beam Headlight.

Convertibles disappeared in the face of possible "roll-over" safety standards in the mid-seventies. The legislation never materialized but the last soft-top was built in 1976. Who built it?
It was the Cadillac Eldorado.

After a six-year hiatus in North America, this company brought the convertible back. Was it Ford, Chrysler, or Pontiac?
Chrysler.

What was the convertible model it introduced in 1982?
The Le Baron Convertible.

In the late twenties and early thirties, the Budd (All-Steel Bodies) Company of Philadelphia developed an advanced car design featuring unitized construction and front-wheel-drive. They were unable to sell the idea to their domestic customers but a visiting European thought it was great and bought it. Who was he?
Andre Citröen. The vehicle — with styling by Bertone — became the classic "French" car, the Citröen Traction Avant.

Andre Citröen ran into financial trouble in 1934. Even with the great success of the Traction Avant introduced that year, the company foundered and was taken over by its major creditor. Who was the new owner?
Michelin.

This classic American car, introduced in 1936, had such unique styling it was patented! What was the car?
The Cord 810, designed by Gordon Buehrig.

What company introduced the "H" slot gearshift pattern in 1902? Was it Ford, Packard, or Hudson?
Packard.

The Kaiser-Darrin DKF-161, designed by Howard Darrin, and standing only 36 inches tall, pioneered a new kind of body fabrication. What was it?
Fiberglas reinforced plastic body.

ENGINEERING & DESIGN

What 1966 U.S. car had a split transmission and chain drive? Clue: it had front-wheel drive.
Olds Toronado.

What company introduced "Oriflow Drive" in 1952?
Dodge.

The first flush-mounted, aerodynamic headlights on a U.S. car appeared in 1984. What was the car: a Cadillac, Lincoln Continental, or Chrysler Imperial?
Lincoln Continental MK. VII.

Charles C. Wakefield was the first to develop an engine oil specifically for high performance uses. What is its name: Veedol, Castrol, or Penzoil?
Castrol.

What does Wakefield's middle initial "C" stand for?
Cheers.

The first diesel-powered production car was the Mercedes 260D of 1936. But the first diesel-powered car to appear in the United States was a 1929 Packard. What diesel engine did it use?
A Cummins Diesel.

Hudson led the way with a new type of bodywork for its 1922 Essex model. What was the innovative feature of this car?
It was the first affordable car with closed bodywork. It finally made the car a year-round proposition.

The Journal of Elemental Locomotion was the first automotive publication. It was introduced in England by Alexander Gordon in 1832, 1849, or 1860?
1832.

What was the "Croisiere Noire" expedition?
The first successful Trans-Sahara crossing by car.

When did the expedition take place: 1920, 1924, or 1926?
1924.

What vehicles did the expedition use: Renault, Citröen, or Mercedes?
Citröen half-tracks.

In 1955 this car was the first to offer a self-levelling, hydro-pneumatic suspension system. Was it Renault, Citröen, or Austin?
The Citröen DS-19.

The last of the ragtops in 1976. But not forever.

143

Messerschmidt and Heinkel were famous for their WWII aircraft. After the war, they both tried their hands at a novel form of transportation. What was it?
The "bubble car", or Kabinenroller. Not much better than glorified, enclosed motorcycles, they had a brief popularity in fuel-starved, post-war Europe.

BMW also had a brief affair with "bubble cars", one they would probably like to forget. What was the Italian make they built under license? *Isetta.*

This Dutch company pioneered an "infinitely-variable belt-drive" to the rear wheels — Variomatic — in the late fifties. What was the company? *DAF.*

Before Daimler or Benz, this inventor from Vienna built a simple automobile with a 2-stroke, single-cylinder engine. With no clutch, it was necessary to lift up the rear wheels in order to start, then drop the vehicle to the ground. The locals were not amused or interested. So he simply dismissed the whole thing as "...a senseless waste of

The unpretentious 1962 DAF, was hiding some innovative driveline technology.

time". Who was the inventor?
Siegfried Marcus.

What year was it: 1864, 1871, or 1880?
1871.

What was unique about the 1937 Waterman Arrowmobile?
It was one of the first of the "flying" automobiles.

1935 saw the introduction of this economy car named after Mickey Mouse. What was it?
The Fiat "Topolino".

The first adjustable driver's seat was offered by this company in 1913. Was the company Cadillac, Maxwell, or Oldsmobile?
Maxwell.

The F.W.D. Company introduced a vehicle with a unique drivetrain in 1908. The company's initials are a clue. What type of vehicle was it?
Four-wheel-drive.

In 1904, this company was the first in the United States to mount the gearshift on the steering column. Was it REO, Sturtevant, or Winton?
Winton.

This British version of a "bubble car" is really more like an egg. The 1960 Scootacar didn't start a trend.

ENGINEERING & DESIGN

This European company started to export to the United States in 1949. In the first year it sold only two cars. What was the company?
Volkswagen.

The rear CHMSL was made mandatory in 1985. What is it?
Centre High Mounted Stop Light.

The last Beetle to be built at the Volkswagen Wolfsburg plant rolled out in 1972, 1974, or 1978?
1974.

Everything in this 1949 Kaiser could be opened. Everything...except the left rear door.

These vehicles successfully challenged the Sahara.

CHAPTER 9 / WHAT'S IN A NAME?

At the turn of the century, backyard inventors were bursting out of barns, cowsheds and hencoops with all manner of horseless contraptions. But after the heady excitement of the first successful test run — perhaps all of fifty feet — the elated inventor was faced with his first really tough question, "Well Jethro, whaddyagonnacallit?"

The first obvious choice was to name it after oneself. Henry Ford did it with distinction, as did Buick, Olds and Chrysler, names that have a solid ring to them and look good on the radiator. Why didn't it work for Ricketts (1902), Boggs (1903), Crock (1909) and Foos (1913)? And if there was any doubt in these cases, it must surely have been obvious — even to his mother — that the Pungs-Finch would not become a household name. In short, success or failure may hang in the balance, which is why so much time, effort and anguish are devoted to the naming game.

You never know where they've been. Some popular model names first appeared elsewhere; sometimes adorning the most unlikely sheet metal. See if you can identify these "original" users?

Skylark	American Bantam
Riviera	Hupmobile
Pacer	Studebaker
Daytona	Edsel

From the top: Hupmobile (1940), American Bantam (1939), Edsel (1958), and Studebaker (1956).

Match these hardtops to their proper bodies:

_____ Bel Air
_____ Holiday
_____ Country Club

From the top: Chevrolet (1950), Oldsmobile (1949), and Nash (1952).

The Ranger was one of eighteen versions of this model launched in 1958. A massive name search was undertaken before introduction, and poet Marianne Moore was asked for submissions. Among her offerings were: Resilient Bullet, Turcotinga, Mongoose Civique, Pastelogram and Utopian Turtletop. But Ford executives were not about to take chances; they called it Edsel.

Match these less-than-household model names with their correct makes:

Mayfair	Studebaker
Carolina	Oldsmobile
Fiesta	Packard
Challenger	Kaiser

From the top: 1951 Packard, 1953 Kaiser, 1953 Oldsmobile, and 1964 Studebaker.

Who made these "fishy" marques: Marlin, Barracuda, and Manta?
AMC Rambler (1965), Plymouth (1964), and Opel (1971).

Name one other manufacturer for each of these model names:

Corsair	Ford and	_____
Concord	AMC and	_____
Executive	Packard and	_____

From the top: Edsel and Henry J (Kaiser), Plymouth, and Pontiac.

What company made Fargo trucks?
Dodge.

Complete these car names:

_____	Corrado
_____	Swift
_____	Allante

From the top: Volkswagen, Suzuki, Cadillac.

You can't keep a good name down. Name one other manufacturer for each of the following cars:

Lark	Studebaker and	_____
Seville	Cadillac and	_____
Falcon	Ford and	_____

From the top: Willys, De Soto, and Willys.

What is the "Rambo-Lambo"?
The Lamborghini LM-002.

See if you can complete these well-known names:

1913 Mercer Raceabout

Type 35, Series J $2600

The Champion Light Car

Mercer power and efficiency are well-known qualities. These features are decidedly emphasized in our new series. The various models offer a MERCER for every reasonable need.

Prices $2600 to $2900

Descriptive literature sent on request.

MERCER MOTOR CARS

MERCER MOTOR CARS

MERCER AUTOMOBILE COMPANY

400 Whitehead Road,   Trenton, N. J.

For a mere $2,600 you could own this Mercer Raceabout in 1913.

WHAT'S IN A NAME?

_____ Crown Victoria
_____ Road King
_____ Ambassador

From the top: Ford, Plymouth, and Nash/AMC.

And what about these?
_____ Astre
_____ Big Boy
_____ Invicta

From the top: Pontiac, Hudson, and Buick.

Match these exotic nameplates to their makers:

Mondial	Lotus
Urraco	Ferrari
Corniche	Lamborghini
Eclat	Rolls-Royce

From the top: Ferrari, Lamborghini, Rolls-Royce, and Lotus.

Some names are so popular, they are used by more than one company, but not usually at the same time. Identify the other companies that used these model names:

Chevrolet Citation
Dodge Phoenix
Willys Eagle
Plymouth Suburban

From the top: Edsel, Pontiac, AMC and Chevrolet, Nash and Chevrolet.

In each case, name the company that used the model names first?

Jeep Comanche
American Motors Matador
Buick Skylark

From the top: International Scout, Dodge, and Hupp.

A 1939 Adler Trumpf

AUTOMANIA

Complete these pickup names:

_____ Scrambler
_____ Sweptside
_____ Speedwagon

From the top: Jeep, Dodge, and REO.

Can you complete these not so common nameplates?

_____ Kapitan
_____ Minx
_____ Doretti

From the top: Opel, Hillman, and Swallow.

And what about these?

_____ Super Snipe
_____ Hyper
_____ Trumpf

From the top: Humber, Lea-Francis, and Adler.

Or these?

_____ Italia
_____ Saratoga

_____ Terraplane

From the top: Hudson ('55), Chrysler ('46), and Essex ('32).

Complete these pickup names:

_____ Apache
_____ Scout Terra
_____ Gentleman Jim

From the top: Chevrolet, International, and GMC.

_____ Hot Shot
_____ Commuter
_____ Encore

From the top: Crosley ('51), Mercury ('67), and Renault-AMC ('84).

Names are coined to attract attention. Complete these attention-getters.

_____ Airflow
_____ Torpedo
_____ Riviera

From the top: Chrysler, Tucker, and Buick.

Aside from looking quite weird, what is the other unusual feature of this 1937 Panhard Dynamique? Clue: note the three windshield wipers.
It had a central driving position.

WHAT'S IN A NAME?

Complete these veteran names:

_____ Raceabout
_____ Speed Wagon
_____ Great Arrow

From the top: Mercer, Reo, and Pierce.

Complete these veteran names:

_____ Raceabout
_____ Speed Six
_____ Great Arrow

From the top: Mercer, Bentley, and Pierce.

What was "The Lost Cause"?
In 1963, Charles Peaslee Farnsley, one-time mayor of Louisville, Kentucky, produced a special upgraded version of the Corvair Monza. Even before orders could be placed, the Corvair was clearly doomed by Nader's book Unsafe at Any Speed hence the name.

What was the "Trifon Special"?
The Chrysler Airflow in its prototype form (1931–33).

How did it get that name?
Named after Chrysler employee Dimitrion Trifon.

What was the Studillac?
Between 1953 and 1955, Bill Frick installed Cadillac V-8 engines into various models of the Studebaker Starliner hardtop.

From 1960 to 1964, this company produced an electric vehicle called the Henney Kilowatt. It used a European compact as its base. Was it a Renault Dauphine, a Volkswagen, or a DKW?
A Renault Dauphine.

Citröen's Traction Avant, beloved of the Parisian "flics".

Some companies seem to prefer the alphabet soup approach to names. Can you identify these "equations"?
XR4Ti
6000LE
323GTX
From the top: Ford Merkur, Pontiac, and Mazda.

And what about these numbers?
300TE
240SX
405Mi
From the top: Mercedes-Benz, Nissan, and Peugeot

More and more car names are being computer-generated. Can you identify these makes?
Integra
Sentra
Supra
From the top: Honda Acura, Nissan, and Toyota.

And what about these "numbers"?
MR 2
740 GLE
635 CSi
From the top: Toyota, Volvo, and BMW.

Identify these late arrivals from the computer "word bank":
_____ Miata
_____ Justy
_____ Lumina
From the top: Mazda, Subaru, and Chevrolet.

What company produced the "Spinto" and "Super Spinto" models in the thirties?
Isotta-Fraschini.

Here are some more "nameless numbers" to identify:
928 S4
135 GLI
9000 CD
From the top: Porsche, Skoda, and Saab.

Complete these not so common names:
_____ Panhard
_____ Aronde
_____ Javelin
From the top: Dyna, Simca, and Jowett (and later AMC).

Complete these "pickup" names:
_____ Caballero
_____ Ranger
_____ Arrow
From the top: GMC, Ford, and Plymouth.

What are "Beemers", "Moggies" and "Spridgets"?
BMWs; Morgans; collectively, Austin Healey Sprites and MG Midgets.

The "Silver Hawk", "Golden Hawk" and "Gran Turismo Hawk" were all marketed by this American manufacturer. Was it Stutz, Buick or Studebaker?
Studebaker.

Called Turicum, these vehicles were the work of Swiss engineer Martin Fischer between 1904 and 1913. What was unusual about these cars?
They were steered by foot pedals.

What does the name Turicum mean?
It is the Latin name for Zurich.

WHAT'S IN A NAME?

In 1905 this company marketed a vehicle that was designed not to exceed the current 20 mph speed limit. What was it called?
The Legalimit.

Who built it?
Rolls-Royce.

Why was the Buick Century, introduced in 1936, so-called?
Its new 320 CID, inline 8-cylinder engine developed 120 horsepower, making it capable of a true 100 mph.

When Daihatsu indicated that they would introduce a new sport utility vehicle in 1990 called the Rocky, they ran into an unusual problem. What was it?
MGM/UA, the producers of Sly Stallone's repetitive Rocky movies objected. After the lawyers were finished, Daihatsu had been given permission to use the name in return for 'valuable considerations'.

Match these unusual monikers to their makers:
Pirate   Jeep
Prosperity Six Franklin
Harlequin   Graham
From the top: Franklin Graham, Jeep.

Why couldn't General Motors market the Nova in Spanish speaking countries?
Because "no va" means "won't go" in Spanish.

How did the Audi get its name?
Dr. August Horch began building cars bearing his name in 1899. A difficult man to work with, he soon fell out with his backers and left to form another company. Legally prevented from using his own name, he solved the problem in an innovative way. The 'horch' in German means 'hear' and so he chose the Latin translation 'audi'. In 1932, Audi, Wanderer, DKW and the original Horch merged to form Auto Union and when Volkswagen took over in 1965 only the Audi name survived.

What do the initials of the British company AC stand for?
Auto Carriers. The company started building 3-wheeler commercial vans in 1904.

What is the significance of the '356' in the Porsche 356 introduced in 1948?
It was the 356th design of the Prosche Design Bureau.

They changed the name to 'Tucker 48' but it didn't help. What was it called before?
The Tucker Torpedo.

ACKNOWLEDGEMENTS

First of all I should like to thank Dennis Morgan, editor of the *Wheels* section of the *Toronto Star*, for giving my *Autotrivia* column a regular home and encouraging me to write this book. Ron Grantz, curator of the National Automotive History Collection of the Detroit Public Library and his staff, were most generous in their help, as was Paul Scupholm, director of the Friends of the Detroit Public Library. All the photographs in *Automania* were meticulously reproduced from original library archives by Bill Bailey. I am also grateful to friend and one-time associate Hugh McCall who agreed to read the original text and made valuable contributions to it. Thanks are also due to Chrysler colleagues A.C. Liebler, M.K. Morrison, Steve Harris, Tom Kowalesky and Ilene Zeldin who provided invaluable advice and assistance. Finally, I would like to thank Lee A. Iacocca for seeing the merit in *Automania* and lending his considerable prestige to the endeavour.

INDEX

INDEX

INDEX